100

THINGS TO DO IN
BOULDER
BEFORE YOU
DIE

Tubing to Work
Photo courtesy of Caroline Colvin

100
THINGS TO DO IN
BOULDER
BEFORE YOU
DIE

● ●

SANDY BORNSTEIN

REEDY PRESS

Library of Congress Control Number: 2022936983

ISBN: 9781681063799

Design by Jill Halpin

All photos were provided by the author unless otherwise noted.

Printed in the United States of America
22 23 24 25 26   5 4 3 2 1

DEDICATION

To Boulder's majestic and tranquil location
that captivated my attention decades ago.

To my husband, Ira, who agreed that a midlife decision to
relocate back to Colorado was worth the gamble. Without this
major upheaval in our family's lives, and his support, decades
later, while he was enduring treatment for glioblastoma, an
incurable brain cancer, this book would not have been possible.

● ●

CONTENTS

• •

Music and Entertainment

• •

Sports and Recreation

• •

● ●

Culture and History

• •

Shopping and Fashion

• •

PREFACE

When was the last time you visited a medium-sized American city that offered an abundance of year-round outdoor adventures, a cross-section of cultural attractions, diverse culinary cuisines, more than 300 days of sunshine every year, and easy access to a regional airport? As an award-winning travel writer, I have traveled throughout the world. I have yet to encounter a place that offered so many perks in a community with a little more than 100,000 residents.

I was introduced to Boulder when I was accepted as an incoming college freshman at the University of Colorado. Decades later, I still recall the first time I approached the city on the Boulder–Denver Turnpike. When our car stopped at the Davidson Mesa lookout point, I instantly appreciated the immense beauty of this remarkable college town. My eyes became fixated on the jagged Flatirons in the background. I was intrigued by the cluster of red-tiled roofs, a signature of the campus' architecture.

Halfway through my freshman year I became engaged to my husband. Either we would endure a long-distance engagement or I would need to transfer to a university located in the city where Ira would be attending law school. Sadly, we left Colorado. In 2000, we made a quality-of-life decision. We relocated our family from suburban Chicago to Colorado, and from that point forward we could enjoy Boulder and the mountains as often as we liked.

• •

Just like people who have grown and matured, Boulder has changed in many ways since my first visit in 1974. While the antiquated Crossroads Mall was updated to a retail center and renamed the Twenty-Ninth Street Mall, the University of Colorado–Boulder campus continued to expand. Pearl Street became a red-brick pedestrian thoroughfare referred to as the Pearl Street Mall. The Hill, a trendy commercial area adjacent to the campus, remains a work in progress as it undergoes redevelopment with the addition of two hotels and a conference center. During this transformation process, Boulder has remained a hub for healthy outdoor living, a mecca for scientific research, and a magnet for artistic endeavors. The city has simultaneously developed a reputation for attracting quality chefs, a wide assortment of microbreweries, and a few distilleries and wineries. Community and university annual events have become increasingly popular.

The pandemic caused many well-known entities to close but also offered an opportunity for new businesses to open. Boulder County faced the indescribable trauma caused by the 2021 Marshall Fire, the most destructive fire in Colorado history. It left more than 1,000 families homeless. The community remarkably rebounded as it faced these adversities.

There are far more than 100 places worth visiting in and around Boulder. To complete the book, I selected a cross-section of locations appealing to locals and visitors along with college students and their parents. Adventuresome spirits can scroll through the Expand Your Horizons suggestions found near the end of the book, while less-active folks can consider items in the

At Your Leisure section. Couples seeking memorable moments can find recommendations for Romantic Encounters. Parents traveling with school-age children may find the Family Fun section useful when planning their daily activities, while people looking to embrace CU spirit can focus on the Stand Shoulder to Shoulder with the Buffaloes attractions. History mavens will be pleasantly surprised to see how Boulder progressed from a mining town to a hippy university town to a health-conscious city to a year-round vacation destination. If you find yourself in Boulder for more than a couple of days, it is imperative that you spend some time exploring the nearby mountains. To learn more about day trips, check the Outside Boulder recommendations.

Welcome to Boulder.

ACKNOWLEDGMENTS

Countless friends, acquaintances, and family members shared their experiences. Their insight opened my eyes to many locations. I also want to single out Kim Farin, Karleen Lewis, and Bailey Burrows from the Boulder Convention and Visitor Bureau, and Teri Takata-Smith and Anna Salim from the Downtown Boulder Partnership. Their cooperation and assistance helped to make this book possible. Also, special thanks to Josh Stevens for extending the contract to write this book. And to the Reedy Publishing team—Barbara Northcott, Chelcie Grant, Renee Letz, and Jill Halpin—who worked together to create this book.

Cheesecake at Jill's Restaurant

FOOD AND DRINK

SEEK OUT LOCAL ITEMS
AT THE BOULDER FARMERS MARKET

From the first weekend in April through the Saturday preceding Thanksgiving, crowds form early on Saturdays between 8 a.m. and 2 p.m. on 13th Street between Canyon Boulevard and Arapahoe Avenue. Approximately 65 "growers only" vendors and locally sourced items are featured each week. All producers must raise or grow whatever they sell at their booths. From exotic mushrooms to the western slope's Palisade peaches to fresh bakery goods, it's hard to leave without something in hand. This marketplace is often singled out as one of the best in Colorado and appears on nationwide lists of outstanding farmers markets. If you are not available on Saturday, consider the scaled-down version on Wednesdays, with around 45 vendors, from 4 p.m. to 7:30 p.m. from early May to early October. The midweek market has live music and a beer garden.

13th Street between Canyon and Arapahoe, 303-910-2236
bcfm.org

TIP

Arrive early. Specialty items may sell out quickly. Consider bringing a large shopping bag to make it easier to carry your purchases.

DRIVE UP THE FOOTHILLS FOR A SCENIC MEAL
AT FLAGSTAFF HOUSE RESTAURANT

The combination of fine dining coupled with spectacular views is a rare commodity. For more than 50 years, the Monette family has served locals celebrating countless milestones as well as first-time visitors who were drawn by the restaurant's impeccable reputation. The amazing panoramic view seen through the oversized restaurant windows or from the tiered outdoor terrace may temporarily distract diners from making their menu choices. Two set-price options—a Chef's Tasting Menu and a Four Course Menu—are boldly listed along with the option of ordering à la carte. The restaurant's French–American cuisine ingredients are locally sourced and rotate during the seasons. Rest assured that their wine service is exemplary, having receiving decades of *Wine Spectator* Grand Awards. Driving up the switchback mountain road can be an adventure for people unfamiliar with quick elevation gains. The memorable experience will conclude with an award-winning (*Forbes* 4 Star and 4 Diamonds by AAA) meal.

1138 Flagstaff Rd., 303-442-4640
flagstaffhouse.com

START YOUR DAY
WITH A SIT-DOWN BREAKFAST

Boulder has numerous menu options that can kick-start your metabolism and energize your body for a full day of activities. Avoid the long lines at The Buff by arriving early to enjoy their hearty entrées, which range from breakfast basics to high-calorie apple pancakes to Southwestern specialties to soups and salads. Grab a seat outside the cozy Walnut Café to enjoy their version of regular and vegetarian options. For an innovative approach to your first meal, drive to North Boulder for a meal at Tangerine. If you have a craving for waffles, include The Waffle Lab on your itinerary. In an old house close to the downtown area you can indulge in New Orleans–style cooking at Lucile's Creole Café. On weekends, set aside time for a leisurely brunch at Boulder Dushanbe Teahouse, the Greenbriar Inn, Jill's Restaurant, The Kitchen American Bistro, or River and Woods.

The Buff
2600 Canyon Blvd.
303-442-9150
buffrestaurant.com

Walnut Café
3073 Walnut St.
303-447-2315
673 S Broadway St.
720-304-8118
walnutcafe.com

Tangerine
2777 Iris Ave.
303-443-2333
Additional locations
in Lafayette and Longmont
tangerineeats.com

The Waffle Lab
1155 13th St.
720-287-4378
Additional locations
in Fort Collins
thewafflelab.com

Lucile's Creole Café
2124 14th St.
303-442-4743
Additional locations
in Longmont, Littleton,
Denver, and Fort Collins
luciles.com

Boulder Dushanbe Teahouse
1770 13th St.
303-442-4993
boulderteahouse.com/
brunch

The Greenbriar Inn
8735 N Foothills Hwy.
303-440-7979
greenbriarinn.com/menus/
sunday-brunch

Jill's Restaurant
900 Walnut St.
720-406-9696
stjulien.com/eat-drink/
jill's-restaurant-and-bistro

The Kitchen American Bistro
1039 Pearl St.
303-544-5973
thekitchenbistros.com/
location/the-kitchen-
bistros-boulder

River and Woods
2328 Pearl St.
303-993-6301
riverandwoodsboulder.com

TAKE TIME TO REBOOT
AT A LOCAL COFFEE SHOP

Coffee mavens seek out the best cafés in town. Beleza is a multi-roaster coffee shop featuring Sweet Bloom coffee, one of the top roasters in Colorado, and will also satisfy the needs of tea lovers with diverse palates. At Alpine Modern Café, on The Hill, you can combine a cup of delicious coffee with a health-conscious meal. Tartines, granola, quinoa bowls, and sandwiches are the main choices. Boxcar Coffee Roaster, on the east end of Pearl Street, roasts their own beans and serves pastries and breakfast sandwiches made onsite. This coffee shop shares space with Cured, a specialty food shop. Another option is to grab a cup of coffee at one of Laughing Goat's three locations. If you want a jolt of caffeine before hiking on a Chautauqua trail, stop in The General Store before you reach the trailhead.

Beleza Coffee Bar
2680 Broadway, 303-955-7028
belezacoffeebar.com

Boxcar Coffee Roasters
1825 B Pearl St., 720-456-7962
boxcarcoffee.com

Alpine Modern Café
904 College Ave., 303-954-0129
alpinemodern.com/cafe

The General Store
Chautauqua, 303-952-1632
chautauqua.com/general-store

Laughing Goat
1709 Pearl St.
2907 55th St.
1720 Pleasant St.
thelaughinggoat.com

EAT WITH CHOPSTICKS
AT ALOY THAI CUISINE

If you are a fan of Asian food, you will have no trouble locating delectable Thai, Vietnamese, Japanese, and Chinese cuisine. The bigger issue is deciding which Asian region is your top choice. Aloy Thai's depth of flavors shined in the "College Town Champs" episode of the Food Network's *Diners, Drive-ins and Dives*. While watching this clip, you can see how the Naka family cooks traditional Thai recipes using a multitude of fresh produce and Thai spices. Items selected on Aloy Thai's diverse traditional menu are customized by dietary preferences. Guests can easily add and subtract plant-based foods, seafood, and meat options. It is also possible to select the degree of spiciness ranging from no spice to medium spicy to Thai hot.

2720 Canyon Blvd., 303-440-2903
aloythai.com

LOOKING FOR A FEW MORE ASIAN FOOD OPTIONS?

Zoe Ma Ma
2010 10th St., 303-545-6262
zoemama.com/boulder

Chez Thuy
2655 28th St., 303-442-1700
chezthuy.com

China Gourmet
3970 N Broadway St., 303-440-3500
chinagourmetmenu.com

Izakaya Amu
1221 Spruce St., 303-440-0807
izakayaamu.com

Flower Pepper
2655 Broadway St., 720-381-1594
flowerpeppereats.com

TREAT YOURSELF TO AN ELEGANT MEAL
AT THE GREENBRIAR INN

For more than 50 years the Greenbriar Inn's extraordinary cuisine has lured people to drive about 15 minutes north into the Boulder countryside to eat made-from-scratch meals prepared with fresh produce, many sourced from their onsite garden. The Greenbriar Inn planted their first garden decades ago, long before the farm-to-table movement became popular. Selections from the bistro and dinner menus can be eaten in the dining room or picnic style on their picturesque grounds. The dinner menu is for heartier appetites. Like other top restaurants, they repeatedly have been recipients of the Best of Award of Excellence from *Wine Spectator*. From oysters on the half shell to artisan cheeses and charcuterie for two to omelets and pan-seared salmon, few restaurants offer such an extensive Sunday brunch menu.

8735 N Foothills Hwy., 303-440-7979
greenbriarinn.com

FIND AUTHENTIC
MEDITERRANEAN CUISINE
AT ASH'KARA

Ash'Kara is a spinoff from the original location in Denver's LoHi neighborhood. Executive chef and co-owner Daniel Asher transplanted his shareable-plate concept permeated with Middle Eastern cuisine to Boulder's Pearl Street Mall. Anyone who has traveled to the region will recognize the spices, the sauces, the appetizers, and the entrées that are part of Mediterranean culinary culture. Asher's strong advocacy for fresh organic ingredients shines through in the presentation of the vegetarian menu options. To fully appreciate a Middle Eastern feast it is best to come with a table full of people and to sample a side, some hummus with wood-fired heirloom grain pita, a dip or two, along with a few tapas and accoutrements. Make sure to leave room for two Israeli favorites, sufganiyot and halvah.

1043 Pearl St., 303-993-5286
ashkarafood.com

EAT ON THE RUN
IN BETWEEN TOURING

On busy touring days, quick lunches become a necessity. To satisfy diverse palates, here is a cross-section of on-the-go food choices. Rush Bowls, launched in Boulder, offers nutrient-dense items packing a punch with an assortment of fruits, vegetables, and proteins. Moe's Bagels can quickly prepare a bagel or build a specialty sandwich. Another option for sandwiches is Snarf's Sandwiches, a chain with Boulder roots. Ethnic foods offer a change of pace. For a selection of empanadas, visit Rincon Argentino. Falafel King Mediterranean Café on Pearl Street is a great option for Middle Eastern pita wraps. At Colorado-based Illegal Pete's, select a handmade Southwestern favorite. If you are craving a Chicago-style hot dog, Mustard's Last Stand can accommodate you as well as your vegetarian companions.

Rush Bowls Boulder—The Hill
1207 13th St., 303-546-9666
rushbowls.com/boulder

Moe's Bagels
2650 Broadway St., 303-444-3252
3267 28th St., 720-406-9000
3075 Arapahoe Ave., 303-442-4427
637 S Broadway St., 720-287-0317
moesbagel.com

Snarf's Sandwiches
2660 Pearl St., 303-444-7766
5340 Arapahoe Ave., 303-444-3404
637 S Broadway St., 303-444-7714
6562 Lookout Rd., 720-622-0107
eatsnarfs.com/pearl-boulder

Rincon Argentino
2525 Arapahoe Ave., 303-442-4133
rinconargentinoboulder.com

Falafel King Restaurant
1314 Pearl St., 303-449-9321
falafelkingfoods.com

Illegal Pete's
1447 Pearl St., 303-440-3955
1124 13th St., 303-444-3055
illegalpetes.com

Mustard's Last Stand
1719 Broadway St., 303-444-5841
mustardslaststandcolorado.com

GET READY
FOR A PICNIC

A bonus to hiking on Boulder trails is the leisure time spent enjoying the scenery while eating a delicious picnic lunch. After a couple hours of hiking, appetites soar. In addition to gear for inclement weather, pack some food in your daypack. Cured specializes in European-style sandwiches and homemade salads and sells several picnic baskets. Meat, fish, and vegetarian subs can be purchased at Half Fast Subs on The Hill. Bowls served with rice or salad and banh mi sandwiches can be picked up at Daikon Banh Mi Shop in the 29th Street Mall. Vegans, vegetarians, carnivores, gluten-free, and the pickiest eaters will find plenty of healthy choices at the Organic Sandwich Company at the corner of 16th and Pearl. Another sure bet for a nutrient-dense menu is Flower Child, part of the nationwide community of Fox Restaurant Concepts, where bowls, salads, and wraps are staple items.

TIP

Dehydration can become a serious issue in arid Front Range communities. Remember to pack plenty of water and to sip throughout the day.

Cured
1825 B Pearl St., 720-389-8096
curedboulder.com

Half Fast Subs
1215 13th St., 303-449-0404
halffastsubs.com

Organic Sandwich Company
1500 Pearl St., 720-639-3986
459 S McCaslin Blvd., Louisville, 720-598-5931
organicsandwichco.com

Daikon Banh Mi Shop
1805 29th St., Ste. 1138, 720-640-4063
daikon.com

Flower Child
2580 Arapahoe Ave., 303-386-8090
iamaflowerchild.com

SATISFY YOUR CRAVING
FOR AUTHENTIC ITALIAN PIZZA
AT PIZZERIA LOCALE

You don't have to travel to Naples, to taste authentic Italian pizza. While in Boulder, you can dine at Pizzeria Locale. The idea to bring Neapolitan-style pizza to Boulder was conceived by the owners of Frasca, a James Beard Award–winning Boulder restaurant. The two restaurants sit side by side on the east end of Pearl Street. Since 2011, the first Stefano Ferrara wood-fired oven in Colorado has baked an untold number of delectable pizzas. Your appetite will be primed with a small starter or salad. Depending on personal preference, choose between the Pizze Bianche (without marinara sauce) and Pizze Rosse (tomato based) selections. Dairy-free and gluten-free food preferences can be accommodated. For a tasty butterscotch dessert, try the budino.

1730 Pearl St., 303-442-3003
Additional locations in Denver
localeboulder.com

A FEW MORE PLACES TO TRY PIZZA

Fringe
2900 Valmont Rd., 303-386-4631
fringepizza.com

Basta
3601 Arapahoe Ave., 303-997-8775
bastaboulder.com

Barchetta
1644 Walnut St., 720-749-4751
barchetta.pizza

Carelli's of Boulder
645 30th St., 303-938-9300
carellis.com

MEET AT THE KITCHEN AMERICAN BISTRO
FOR AN UPBEAT MEAL

While it is possible to enjoy a similar meal outside of Boulder, the Kitchen Restaurant Group concept originated in Boulder in 2004. Like many other noteworthy Boulder restaurants, The Kitchen adheres to the popular farm-to-table concept with an emphasis on sustainable and locally sourced ingredients. The intimate dining room matches perfectly with the limited menus for brunch, lunch, and dinner. The crispy cauliflower, a signature dish, appears on all three menus. The roasted mushroom, leeks, and parmesan quiche is a standout for brunch. Even though the options may be relatively few, carnivores, pescatarians, and vegetarians will be satisfied with the selection, the quality of the preparation, and the personable service. With a limited number of seats, it is advisable to book a reservation.

1039 Pearl St., 303-544-5973
thekitchenbistros.com/location/the-kitchen-bistros-boulder

UNABLE TO BOOK A RESERVATION? TRY ...

Oak at Fourteenth
1400 Pearl St.
303-444-3622
oakatfourteenth.com

River and Woods
2328 Pearl St.
303-993-6301
riverandwoodsboulder.com

Salt
1047 Pearl St.
303-444-7258
saltboulder.com

Blackbelly
1606 Conestoga St.
303-247-1000
blackbelly.com

Boulder Cork
3295 30th St.
303-443-9505
bouldercork.com

CELEBRATE
AT FRASCA FOOD AND WINE

From its inception in 2004, Frasca Food and Wine has been touted as a top dining spot. The combined skills of Chef Lachlan MacKinnon-Patterson and master sommelier Bobby Stuckey have naturally led to James Beard Awards in 2008, 2013, and 2019. The restaurant's cuisine mirrors the culinary scene in Friuli Venezia Giulia, a sub-alpine region in northeast Italy. Foodies will be in heaven when they read through the four-course fixed-price menu and a secondary chef's tasting menu with optional wine pairings. Both menus change frequently. Few guests opt to order à la carte. Stuckey adeptly meets the challenge of pairing wine at tables with mixed personalities and food choices. Try Frico Caldo, a traditional Friulian pancake made of crushed Yukon gold potatoes, Montasio cheese, and onions, one of Frasca's signature dishes.

1738 Pearl St., 303-442-6966
frascafoodandwine.com

LOOKING FOR MORE FINE-DINING EXPERIENCES?

Corrida
1023 Walnut, St., 303-444-1333
corridaboulder.com

Steakhouse No. 316
1922 13th St., 720-729-1922
steakhouse316.com

Frank's Chophouse
921 Walnut St., 303-444-1295
frankschophouseboulder.com

EAT LOX AND BAGELS
AT ROSENBERG'S
BAGELS & DELICATESSEN

People who were raised on traditional Jewish bagels know that the authentic version is boiled before it is baked. They can instantly taste the difference between a mass-produced baked bagel and a bagel prepared the old-fashioned way. Owner Joshua Pollack brought traditional bagels to Denver, in 2014 when he opened his Five Points neighborhood deli. Rosenberg's bagels adhere to the boiled method and take the process one step further by using a filtration system mimicking the mineral content of New York City water. Pollack's success led to the opening of the Boulder location on The Hill. Bagels may draw people in to the restaurant, but many order the conventional and innovative deli options along with drinks slected from an assortment of coffee, tea, and alcoholic beverages.

1262 College Ave., 720-639-9129
rosenbergsbagels.com

ADMIRE THE DEPTH OF ITALIAN COOKING
AT CARELLI'S OF BOULDER

Boulder and Denver media outlets have consistently singled out Carelli's of Boulder as one of Boulder's best Italian restaurants. Unlike other restaurants focusing on a specific region, Carelli's consistently serves quality, made-from-scratch entrées with mostly organic ingredients, originating from both northern and southern Italian cuisines. For frequent diners, a seasonal daily special is a welcomed change of pace. First-timers may struggle selecting an entrée from the extensive list of foods. While homemade pastas are extremely tempting, the fish, veal, and steak entrées are equally enticing. Calzoni, hot paninis, and artisan pizza round out the possibilities. A separate menu is available for people requesting gluten-free foods. Dessert lovers will be thrilled with Carelli's crespelle (Italian crepes). Their 12 varieties range from a simple lemon and sugar option to an elaborate crepe that resembles Bananas Foster. Parking is free and plentiful in the William's Village Shopping Center.

643 30th St., 303-938-9300
carellis.com

RELISH FRESH SEAFOOD
AT JAX FISH HOUSE & OYSTER BAR

Landlocked locations face a challenge in getting fresh fish daily. Few inland places can compete with the convenience and natural advantages associated with a coastline address. But decades of relationships with fish purveyors ensure quality fresh fish options at Jax's. Chef Sheila Lucero's culinary skills garnered from her education at the Colorado Art Institute and hands-on experience, coupled with an emphasis on procuring the most sustainable ocean seafood, has netted her several dining awards. Her activism has led to an appearance before the US Congress to discuss environmental policies. Jax Fish House is the first restaurant to be certified by the Monterey Bay Seafood Watch, an innovative organization setting standards for the global sustainable seafood movement. While many patrons come for the oyster, shrimp, calamari, and octopus starters or fresh soups, others come for Jax favorites emphasizing seasonal catches.

938 Pearl St., 303-444-1811
jaxfishhouse.com/boulder

DINE AT AN ICON OF GLOBAL FRIENDSHIP
AT THE BOULDER DUSHANBE TEAHOUSE

Both the exterior and interior of the Dushanbe Teahouse stand as a testament to the relationship between the City of Boulder and Dushanbe, the capital of Tajikistan. To celebrate their sister-city tie, artisans from Tajikistan created an extraordinary teahouse near Boulder Creek. Inside this remarkable Boulder landmark, visitors eat brunch, lunch, afternoon tea, dim sum teatime, dinner, and/or dessert while admiring the superlative craftsmanship on the walls, pillars, and ceiling. Locals and people coming from outside Boulder frequently take advantage of the catering service to hold special events inside the teahouse. Many of the recipes' organic ingredients are harvested from the nearby Three Leaf Farm, an entity servicing multiple Boulder restaurants. Vegetarians and tea lovers will be thrilled by the choices.

1770 13th St., 303-442-4993
boulderteahouse.com

PREGAME
AT A LOCAL BAR

Students 21 years and older don't wait for a special occasion to drink. Boulder's bars are frequently packed with people, especially when there is a University of Colorado (CU) Buffalo football game. The Dark Horse, a casual dive bar with reasonably priced food, and The Sink, a funky bar on The Hill known for its burgers and pizza, have been Boulder staples for decades, drawing a mixture of both students and alumni. Long Island iced teas and margaritas are popular at Half Fast Subs on The Hill. Some of the best selections of margaritas can be ordered at the Rio Grande Mexican Restaurant, My Neighbor Felix, and Illegal Pete's. Strobe lights and arcade games draw some to Press Play, while playing pool and craft beer entices others to visit Sundown Saloon.

World Famous Dark Horse
2922 Baseline Rd., 303-442-8162
darkhorsebar.com

The Sink
1165 13th St., 303-444-7465
thesink.com

Half Fast Subs
1215 13th St., 303-449-0404
halffastsubs.com

Rio Grande
Mexican Restaurant
1101 Walnut St., 303-444-3690
riograndemexican.com

My Neighbor Felix
901 Pearl St., 303-376-9552
myneighborfelix.com/boulder

Illegal Pete's
1447 Pearl St., 303-440-3955
illegalpetes.com/location/illegal-petes-boulder-pearl-street
1124 13th St., 303-444-3055
illegalpetes.com/location/illegal-petes-boulder-the-hill

Press Play
1005 Pearl St., 720-508-4916
pressplaybar.com

Sundown Saloon
(a.k.a. The Downer)
1136 Pearl St., 303-449-4987
boulderdowntown.com/go/sundown-saloon

LOOKING FOR SUSHI?
TRY JAPANGO

Landlocked Boulder adeptly addresses the needs of Boulderites and visitors who thrive on raw-fish entrées. Authentic maki, temaki, nigiri, and sashimi are easy to find throughout the community. Japango is the place to go for traditional and innovative creations along with an indoor and outdoor ambience that is hard to match. People-watchers prefer sitting outside to view the Pearl Street Mall action, while most dine inside for lunch and dinner. Substantial lunchtime bento boxes are a great introduction to the diversity of the menu. The lunch menu is similar to the dinner offerings. Happy hour specials are enticing for people on a budget and are extended to all day on Mondays. From classic and innovative cocktails to whiskeys and sake, the bar is ready to pour everyone's favorites.

1136 Pearl St., 303-938-0330
boulderjapango.com

TIP
Take time to review the detailed menu and consider eating family style so you can sample as much as possible.

HERE ARE THREE MORE PLACES FOR SUSHI

Sushi Zanmai
1221 Spruce St., 303-440-0733
sushizanmai.com

Hapa Sushi Grill & Sake Bar
1117 Pearl St., 303-963-9667
hapasushi.com/pages/pearl-street-in-boulder

Motomaki
1600 28th St., 720-575-3318
motomaki.com/location/boulder

PICK UP
ARTISAN BREADS
AND BAKERY GOODS
AT MOXIE

Moxie Bread Co. takes pride in being a local, independent bakery with a commitment to using organic, unprocessed grains from family farms when baking bread and pastries. Due to their slow fermentation process, you are less likely to experience many of the inflammatory responses associated with processed white flour. Breads made with heirloom grains are a top choice, but make sure to save room for a few delectable pastries. The original Moxie in nearby Louisville opened in 2015. The success in Louisville led to the opening of a second location in Boulder, where it is possible to purchase grains from their mill, and the building of a third location in Lyons. In 2018 and 2019, Andy Clark, owner and baker, was recognized by James Beard as a semifinalist in the bakery category.

TIP
To avoid the likelihood of waiting in line, consider ordering online before heading to the bakery.

MOXIE LOCATIONS
4593 Broadway St., 303-903-9961
641 Main St., Louisville, 720-420-9616
355 Main St., Lyons, 720-775-5589
moxiebreadco.com

A FEW MORE LOCAL BAKERIES

Breadworks
2644 Broadway St., 303-444-5667
boulderbreadworks.com

Spruce Confections and Spruce Cafe
767 Pearl St., 303-449-6773
4684 Broadway St., 303-449-5819
4740 Pearl Pkwy., 303-862-6931
3775 Discovery Dr. (on campus)
spruceconfections.com

The Village Nosh
417 Dewey Ave., 404-474-7862
thevillagenosh.com

Shamane's Bakery and Café
2825 Wilderness Pl., 303-417-9338
shamanesbakery.com/home

Boulder Baked
5290 Arapahoe Ave., 303-444-4999
boulderbaked.com

GET YOUR CHOCOLATE FIX
AT PIECE LOVE & CHOCOLATE

From breakfast to dinnertime, chocoholics will salivate upon entering this west-side Pearl Street mecca for chocolate. One's senses are in overdrive while processing the displays and simultaneously breathing in the essence of chocolate permeating the air. If your timing is right, you may get to sample a remnant from the latest batch of homemade truffles. Selecting from a display case filled with dozens of truffles can be challenging. Many are infused with standard ingredients, but more adventuresome souls can try the sweet tomato and basil or the Maya spice with roasted cascabel, ancho, and habañero chilis. The classic version is made with 85 percent bittersweet Valrhona Albinao chocolate. Dairy-free truffles are available. Chocoholics can also sip on specialty drinks or enroll in an upcoming chocolate-making, baking, or pastry class.

805 Pearl St., 303-449-4804
pieceloveandchocolate.com

THREE MORE PLACES TO INDULGE IN CHOCOLATE

Kilwins
1430 Pearl St., 303-442-1940
kilwins.com/stores/kilwins-boulder

Moksha
2746 47th St., 720-648-8893
mokshachocolate.com

Lift Chocolate
6395 Gunpark Dr., Ste. R, 303-447-1001
liftchocolates.com

BECOME NOSTALGIC
AT THE SINK

Over a span of nearly 100 years, The Sink has endured a series of owners all catering to the college crowd, the Boulder community, and a steady stream of visitors and CU alums. Each permutation added another layer to its history and ultimately caught the attention of President Barak Obama, who visited in 2012. The Sink was also featured on the Food Network's *Diners, Drive-Ins and Dives*. The facelifts may have adapted to the times, but part of the ambiance remains with the colorful walls and a ceiling covered in graffiti. The menu has kept pace with current times and features burgers made from local, grass-fed beef; a selection of half- and full-sized salads; and standard college favorites like tacos, nachos, sliders, buffalo wings, and pizza.

1165 13th St., 303-444-7465
thesink.com

SUPPORT A COMMUNITY
DEVASTATED BY THE MARSHALL FIRE BY DINING AT A LOUISVILLE RESTAURANT

At the end of 2021, sections of unincorporated Boulder County and the nearby towns of Superior and Louisville were devastated by a wind-driven fire that left more than 1,000 families homeless. To support these communities, drive just 10 miles southeast of Boulder to Louisville to sample their diverse cuisine. Try Via Toscana for a hearty, multi-course Tuscan-style dinner or à la carte options. Another multi-course option is the family-owned Busaba restaurant, serving authentic Thai food. Their extensive nutrient-dense menu can be customized. Fondue lovers will jump at the chance to have a romantic meal at the Melting Pot. The Huckleberry embraces the farm-to-table concept by using locally produced and organic ingredients. End the day with handcrafted ice cream scooped at Sweet Cow.

Via Toscana Ristorante
356 McCaslin Blvd., Louisville, 303-604-6960
viatoscana.com

Busaba
133 S McCaslin Rd., Louisville, 303-665-0330
4800 Baseline Rd., 720-350-4927 (takeout only)
busabaco.com

The Melting Pot
732 Main St., Louisville, 303-666-7777
meltingpot.com/louisville-co

The Huckleberry
700 Main St., Louisville, 303-666-8020
thehuckleberry.com

Sweet Cow
637 Front St., Louisville, 303-666-4269
Additional locations in Boulder and Denver
sweetcowicecream.com

TURN INTO
A BEER CONNOISSEUR
DURING A BREWERY TOUR

To get a small sampling of the almost two dozen breweries in Boulder, reserve a brew tour. By partnering with Avery Brewing, Upslope Brewing, Sanitas Brewing, West Flanders Brewing, The Post Brewing, Crystal Springs Brewing, and Boulder Beer Co., Boulder Brew Tours offers a behind-the-scenes two-to-three-hour walking tour of three breweries. Custom bus tours accommodate two to 16 individuals who want to select their four-to-five-hour itinerary. Tour bicyclists who are comfortable combining beer tasting and cycling can check out Beyond Boulder Bike Adventures' Bike-N-Brews Cruise. Prior to COVID some breweries ran tours upon request and on a regular schedule. As Boulder adjusts in the aftermath of COVID, it is best to check local brewery websites for updates. For a current list of Boulder's breweries, wineries, distilleries, and cideries, check out this website page—bouldercoloradousa.com/food-and-drink/breweries-wineries-distilleries

Boulder Brew Tours
lee@boulderbrewtours.com, 303-522-3236
boulderbrewtours.com

Beyond Boulder Bike Adventures
2005 18th St., 720-772-9659
beyondboulderadventures.com

EXPERIENCE HIMALAYAN FOOD
AT SHERPA'S

A couple of decades ago, Pemba Sherpa brought his native Himalayan culture and cuisine to Boulder. Before arriving in Boulder, Pemba Sherpa grew up in Nepal and was a well-known professional mountain guide. In a converted house in the west end of the downtown area, you can sample traditional food items from Nepal, Tibet, and India. Guests have the option of dining in one of the cozy rooms or sitting in the outside patio area. Asian chefs use fresh ingredients, regional spices, and family recipes to deliver authentic Himalayan food to customers. Heartier appetites can consider starting with an appetizer or soup. Don't forget to order the nann baked in a Tandoor oven. The intensity of the entrée spices can be adjusted to accommodate personal preferences.

825 Walnut St., 303-440-7151
sherpas-restaurant.com

SAVOR INNOVATIVE SOUTHWESTERN CUISINE
AT MY NEIGHBOR FELIX

The term "Southwestern cuisine" includes the blending of several culinary styles ranging from those of early Spanish settlers to cowboys, Native Americans, and Mexicans. For decades, Boulder chefs have personalized their approach to preparing classic dishes using the three sisters—corn, squash, and beans. My Neighbor Felix, a newer member of the Boulder food scene, takes a Mexican approach for its brunch, lunch, dinner, and dessert menus, favoring locally sourced ingredients. With an abundance of familiar and creative options at a range of price points, even the pickiest eater will be satisfied. Lunch-goers can try the two-dish combo to double their tasting pleasure. Happy hour specials, Taco Tuesdays, and a CU Student Special Brunch attract the college crowd. Specialty margaritas and craft cocktails, along with the 56-ounce shared margarita, are popular alcoholic beverages.

901 Pearl St., 303-376-9552
myneighborfelix.com/boulder

TRY SOME MORE
TRIED-AND-TRUE SOUTHWESTERN MENUS

Efrains
1630 63rd St., 303-440-4045
efrainsrestaurant.com

Centro Mexican Kitchen
950 Pearl St., 303-442-7771
centromexican.com

Rio Grande Mexican Restaurant
1101 Walnut St., 303-444-3690
riograndemexican.com/locations/boulder

T/ACO
1175 Walnut St., 303-443-9468
tacocolorado.com

Santo
1265 Alpine Ave., 303-442-6100
santoboulder.com

MIX CUISINES
AT AVANTI F & B BOULDER
A COLLECTIVE EATERY

For a dining venue that can meet the needs of a diverse group of people under one roof, Boulderites choose Avanti F & B. This collective eatery offers many choices. On the first floor, diners can choose from five restaurants—Boychik (Mediterranean), Quiero Arepas (Venezuelan), Rooted Craft Kitchen (American), Pig and Tiger (Taiwanese), and Rye Society (Contemporary Delicatessen). They can also order coffee and breakfast items from Lost City Coffee or have an alcoholic beverage from the bar. Take the elevator or stairs to enjoy a panoramic view from the outside decks, or sit inside to eat pizza at New Yorksee and drink at the bar. Snag a seat for the monthly comedy show or participate in the Stampede Rooftop Party when the CU Pep Band plays a 15-minute set during the CU Football season.

1401 Pearl St., 720-343-7757
boulder.avantifandb.com

TIP
Don't leave without going upstairs. The terrace is a fun area offering views of the mountains and surrounding area.

Boychik
boychikkitchen.com

Quiero Arepas
quieroarepas.com

Rooted Craft Kitchen
rootedcraftkitchen.com

Pig and Tiger
pigandtiger.co

Rye Society
ryesociety.com

Lost City Coffee
lostcitydenver.com

New Yorksee
newyorkese1.com

RE-ENERGIZE
AT JILL'S RESTAURANT AND BISTRO

Jill's Restaurant and Bistro defies the commonly held belief that locals never eat at a hotel restaurant. Unlike most hotel restaurants that serve mediocre food and fail to capture the residents' attention, Jill's stands out as one of the best places to eat contemporary cuisine made with organic ingredients. On weekends, hotel guests and locals flock to Jill's for its comprehensive weekend brunch menu. The versatile daily offerings for lunch and dinner appeal to vegetarians, pescatarians, and carnivores alike. A wood stone fired pizza can be shared along with a nutrient-dense salad or soup. Sandwiches and burgers will suffice for others. It is also possible to create a three- or four-course feast by selecting an appetizer, salad, entrée, and/or dessert. Add another layer to your evening by attending one of the St. Julien Hotel & Spa's live musical performances promoted on the hotel's website.

900 Walnut St., 720-406-9696
stjulien.com/eat-drink

FOUR MORE
VEGETARIAN-FRIENDLY RESTAURANTS

Flower Child
2580 Arapahoe Ave., #110
303-386-8090
iamaflowerchild.com

Zeal
3101 Pearl St., 720-940-3640
zealfood.com/boulder

Thrive
1509 Arapahoe Ave., 720-616-7785
thrive-boulder.com

Native Food Café
1675 29th St., 303-442-0213
nativefoods.com

SAMPLE
FARM-TO-TABLE FOODS
CREATED BY CHEF ERIC SKOKAN

By successfully combining organic farming with dining opportunities serving regional, in-season cuisine, Eric and Jill Skokan have enriched Boulder's farm-to-table restaurant scene. In 2022, Skokan's culinary contributions were rewarded when he became a James Beard finalist for best chef of the mountain region. A 425-acre organic Boulder County farm is the hub. Year round, their Farm Stand sells local produce and items made within 30 miles of Boulder. Boulder County Farmer Market is another place to find their products. Bramble & Hare, in the historic downtown area, serves a hearty three-course meal showcasing some of the farm's incredible resources in a relaxed and welcoming setting. A drive through Longmont's rolling countryside to Black Cat Farm Table Bistro offers a distinctive culinary adventure. The unique menus depend on the day's harvest. To accommodate a year-round dining experience, guests cluster in weather-resistant, glass-enclosed cabanas outfitted with fans, wood stoves, and heaters.

Black Cat Farm Table Bistro
9889 N 51st St., Longmont
303-444-5500
blackcatboulder.com

Bramble & Hare
1970 13th St., 303-444-9110
brambleandhare.com

Farm Stand
4975 Jay Rd., 303-444-5500

Boulder County Farmers Market
13th Street between Arapahoe
Avenue and Canyon Boulevard
bcfm.org

SAY CHEERS
WITH A SPECIALTY DRINK

With an eclectic bar scene, Boulder meets the needs of its diverse public. Cocktails are dependent on the combination of ingredients. James Lee, an award-winning mixologist, displays his talents making innovative craft cocktails at The Bitter Bar. Tropical drinks are your best bet at the Jungle. In the basement of the Hotel Boulderado, be prepared for an underground speakeasy-inspired cocktail. Time your arrival so you can be seated before sundown on Corrida's rooftop for a romantic drink. Beer lovers will be overwhelmed by the options. Local sources give a thumbs up to Kettle and Spoke, Twisted Pine Brewery, Sanitas Brewing Company, and Backcountry Pizza & Tap House. Sit on West End Tavern's heated outdoor patio to consume craft beer and whiskey while ordering from their extensive menu.

The Bitter Bar
835 Walnut St., 303-442-3050
thebitterbar.com

Jungle
2018 10th St., cassidy@jungletiki.com
jungletiki.com

License # 1 in the Hotel Boulderado
2115 13th St., 303-442-4560
license1boulderado.com

Corrida
1020 Walnut St., 303-444-1333
corridaboulder.com

Kettle and Spoke Brewery
2500 47th St., 720-505-4370
kettleandspoke.com

Twisted Pine Brewing Co.
3201 Walnut St., 303-786-9270
twistedpinebrewing.com

Sanitas Brewing Company Tap Room
3550 Frontier Ave., 303-442-4130
sanitasbrewing.com/tap-room

Backcountry Pizza & Tap House
2319 Arapahoe Ave., 303-449-4285
backcountrypizzaandtaphouse.info

West End Tavern
926 Pearl St., 303-444-3535
thewestendtavern.com

Boulder Creek Festival
Photo courtesy of Boulder Creek Festival

MUSIC
AND ENTERTAINMENT

ATTEND
THE UNIVERSITY OF COLORADO
BOULDER INTERNATIONAL FILM SERIES

While many traditional movie theaters have seen declining attendance in recent years, more than 20,000 movie lovers flock to the 400-seat Muenzinger Auditorium and the 200-seat Visual Arts Complex each year to preview premiere movies and to watch restored 35mm classics. Few places nowadays offer reel-to-reel projection of rare prints on 35mm film. Take time to review the online schedule. Each film is shown only once. Since the 1940s, the International Film Series has brought a variety of special events, film festivals, and award-winning filmmakers to the campus. Don't look for concessions, because none are sold. Proper decorum is ensured by ushers who discourage cellphone usage and texting. Patrons need to show up early since tickets go on sale just 30 minutes prior to showtime.

1905 Colorado Ave., 303-492-1531
internationalfilmseries.com

WATCH LIVE PERFORMANCES
IN THE MACKY AUDITORIUM CONCERT HALL AT THE UNIVERSITY OF COLORADO

Since its debut in 1922, the Macky Auditorium Concert Hall has hosted an abundance of university and community programs. Early on, the 2,040-seat auditorium attracted well-known musicians like Benny Goodman and Harry Belafonte. Architectural mavens and historians will be attracted to its two massive towers built in the Neo-Gothic style. This structure is part of the Norlin Quadrangle Historic District. It is currently the home to the CU Music Department—the CU Music Band, the CU Symphony Orchestra, the Takács Quartet, the CU Opera, the CU Jazz programs, faculty performances, and student recitals. An assortment of other university-sponsored events are also hosted in this concert hall. Tickets can be purchased online for Boulder Philharmonic Orchestra performances, the Boulder Ballet, the Colorado MahlerFest, and the Greater Boulder Youth Orchestra, as well as for events featuring national and international vocalists, choirs, musicians, composers, dance companies, and Grammy Award–winning artists.

1595 Pleasant St., 303-492-8423
colorado.edu/macky

CATCH A MOVIE OR PERFORMANCE
AT BOULDER THEATER

Walking down 14th Street, you cannot miss the dated marquee advertising an upcoming event. Looking closer, one can see traces of the structure's 1930s Art Deco remodeling. After being constructed as an opera house in 1906, the theater served many purposes—live performance venue, silent and talkie film theater, venue for private events, and concert hall. The space has also been rented for weddings, conferences, and meetings. The theater's bookings were temporarily put on hold during the height of the pandemic. From comedy shows to audio-visual experiences to musical performances to the Boulder International Film Festival, the Boulder Theater has recaptured its status as a place to appreciate cultural arts. Tickets for its limited seating of less than 1,000 are available online at Z2 Entertainment.

2032 14th St., 303-786-7030
bouldertheater.com

DRIVE TO MORRISON
FOR A MEMORABLE
RED ROCKS CONCERT

Nestled into the red rocks at 6,450 feet above sea level is the world's only naturally occurring and acoustically perfect open-air amphitheater. This National Historic Landmark in Morrison holds a little more than 9,500 visitors who divide their attention between admiring the rugged red rock terrain, staring at the stars, and relaxing in the serene foothills while listening to world-renowned performers. During its 75-plus years of history, this musical venue has adapted to the times. The 1960s brought the Beatles, Johnny Cash, and Jimi Hendrix, while the 1970s showcased the talents of John Denver and the Grateful Dead. Before the pandemic put a moratorium on live performances, Lionel Richie, Diana Ross, and Stevie Wonder graced the stage. The Red Rocks website highlights the upcoming shows.

18300 W Alameda Pkwy., Morrison, 720-865-2494
redrocksonline.com

TIP
Allow extra time to park for popular concerts, and keep in mind that traffic tends to move slowly after concerts. If you are hungry, you can check out the restaurants in the nearby town of Golden. visitgolden.com/restaurants

UNWIND BY LISTENING TO LIVE MUSIC
AT THE FOX THEATRE ON THE HILL

The Fox Theatre has been a landmark on The Hill for decades. While college students and younger people can recall attending premier concerts, older residents and alums remember the popular movies they watched on the big screen from the 1960s to the early 1990s. Because of the theater's relatively small capacity and state-of-the-art sound system, many experts feel that its atmosphere promotes an extraordinary musical experience. In 2021, the Fox Theatre was inducted into the Colorado Music Hall of Fame. The theater successfully regrouped after the pandemic shutdowns. The calendar started to fill up with an array of local, national, and international musical talent. Check the Z2 Entertainment website for available tickets, and remember that parking is limited on The Hill.

1135 13th St., 303-447-0095
z2ent.com/venues-we-book/fox-theatre-venue

GATHER UNDER THE STARS
AT A COLORADO SHAKESPEARE FESTIVAL PERFORMANCE

While taking the CU campus self-guided tour, you will walk past a well-preserved outdoor theater built in the late 1930s. It was named after Professor Mary Rippon (1850–1935), the first CU female professor and the first woman in the US to teach at a state university. The tradition of using this venue for Shakespeare performances dates to World War II, when the indoor University Theatre was being used by the Department of the Navy. Annual Shakespeare performances during the summer months began in 1958. Since then, the Colorado Shakespeare Festival has become a popular summer event showcasing a selection of Shakespeare's notable works. Tickets are available at the CU Presents website. Performances will not be cancelled unless there are threatening weather conditions.

Mary Rippon Outdoor Theatre, 303-492-8008
colorado.edu/theatredance/news-events/events/colorado-shakespeare-festival

---

TIP
Umbrellas are not permitted, but raingear is a must.

BE INSPIRED
BY A CHAUTAUQUA EVENT

Chautauqua hosts some of Boulder's finest cultural and educational programs featuring local, national, and international talent. The Community House, also known as the "living room," was built in 1918 and winterized in the 1990s. Smaller concerts, films, lectures, workshops, and classes are held in this building offering first-come, first-served seating. The Auditorium, a more rustic barn-like structure, launched its inaugural season in 1898 and is used as a venue from May through September. It accommodates more than 1,000 guests, and seating ranges from padded chairs to theater seats to wooden benches. Be mindful of the outdoor temperature. This historic structure does not have air-conditioning or heat. Check the website for upcoming dates for modern and classical performances, the Colorado Music Festival, film festivals, dance recitals, art exhibits, and notable speakers.

900 Baseline Rd., 303-440-7666
coloradomusicfestival.org

DANCE, DINE, AND DRINK
AT A BANDS ON THE BRICKS CONCERT

Summer concerts usually go hand in hand with a hefty price tag. But since 1997 fans have flocked to Boulder's Pearl Street Mall for free Bands on the Bricks Concerts. This not-to-be-missed event draws approximately 2,000 people ready to dance under the stars and eat while they listen to some of Colorado's best performers. The outdoor beer/wine/margarita garden was expanded recently to encompass a larger portion of the block. Proceeds from the sale of alcohol benefit Downtown Boulder Community Initiatives, a 501(c)(3) organization and the producer of the event. Up and down the Pearl Street Mall, concert-goers can grab a bite to eat from food carts serving everything from tacos to pizza. Options are plentiful for nearby takeout foods and sit-down restaurants.

1300 Block of Pearl St., 303-449-3774
boulderdowntown.com/events/bands-on-the-bricks

SAVE THE DATE
FOR A BOULDER ANNUAL EVENT

Boulder events open the door to local food, art appreciation, and live music. In the spring, the spotlight shines on Boulder Arts Week, when the community recognizes creativity. The Bluebird Music Festival is a two-day, intimate, indie rock folk event held at the Macky Auditorium in April to support the Future Arts Foundation. As the Boulder Bach Festival has matured, it has modified its repertoire to include baroque, classical, and romantic musical works. Kick off Memorial Day weekend at the Boulder Creek Festival and later enjoy the end of summer at the three-day Boulder Fall Fest in mid-September. Since 1995, Open Studio Tours has connected the public with local artists. Foodies are attracted to Boulder County Restaurant Week. Additional events are available on the Boulder Convention Visitor Bureau site.

Boulder Arts Week
boulderartsweek.org

Boulder Fall Fest
boulderdowntown.com/fall-fest

Bluebird Music Festival
bluebirdmusicfestival.org

Open Studios Tour
openstudios.org/open-studios-tour

Boulder Bach Festival
boulderbachfestival.org

Restaurant Week
firstbiteboulder.com

Boulder Creek Festival
bouldercreekfest.com

Boulder Colorado Convention &
Visitor Bureau
bouldercoloradousa.com/events/
annual-events

TAP YOUR FOOT DURING A MUSICAL PERFORMANCE
AT ST. JULIEN HOTEL & SPA

If you enter the St. Julien Hotel & Spa from Wednesday to Saturday evenings in the summer or from Thursday to Saturday evenings the rest of the year, you will have the opportunity to listen to a revolving group of top-notch musicians. Popular local performers appear multiple times a year. This complimentary hotel service introduces a stellar assortment of solo musicians and ensembles ranging from jazz to swing to bossa nova to New Orleans funk. In the cooler months, the evening events are held near the lobby's fireplace from 6 p.m. to 9 p.m. When the weather conditions permit an outdoor venue, the location shifts to the gazebo area. Restaurant and bar service is available to those attending these performances.

900 Walnut St., 720-406-9696
stjulien.com/things-to-do/calendar

OTHER PLACES FOR LIVE MUSIC

Friday Night Jazz
at the Boulderado Hotel
2115 13th St., 303-442-4344
boulderado.com/friday-night-jazz

The Laughing Goat Coffeehouse
1709 Pearl St., contact@
thelaughinggoat.com
thelaughinggoat.com

Trident Booksellers and Café
940 Pearl St., 303-443-3133
tridentcafe.com/events

The Bluebird Supper Club
720-440-4975
bluebirdsupperclub.com

VIEW A MULTIDISCIPLINARY EVENT
AT THE DAIRY ARTS CENTER

The 42,000-square-foot Dairy Arts Center is Boulder County's largest multidisciplinary art center. The original milk-processing facility was reconfigured decades ago into a multidisciplinary venue to showcase artists and live performances. Out-of-towners are drawn to the center's award-winning visual arts programs, four art galleries, and the Boedecker Theater, also known as Boe, Boulder's only art house cinema. The visual arts program is anchored to 27 annual art exhibitions and receptions held in four separate galleries. Visual art workshops and programs for children, teens, and adults coincide with these rotating, juried art shows. The Boedecker Theater connects Boulder to national art house special features, the New York Film Critics national screenings, and live opera and ballet performances streamed from around the world. Talk-backs after some movies and 12:30 p.m. child-friendly movies on Saturdays are trending.

2590 Walnut St., 303-440-7826
thedairy.org

BE ENTERTAINED
AT ɛTOWN HALL

For more than three decades, eTown has been a vital element of Boulder's music and environmental education scene. For its efforts, it was recognized by the Colorado Music Hall of Fame in 2021. Nick and Helen Forster, a husband-and-wife team, run this nationally syndicated radio broadcast/podcast, multimedia, and events production company from a rehabbed former 1922 church that was converted into a multipurpose, energy-efficient, and solar-powered building. Their radio musical performances have included hundreds of top recording artists along with notable activists. The programs have also singled out inspiring individuals who try to address social issues. Doubling as a social and environmental hub for community events, eTown hosts monthly performances for approximately 200 participants. Check their website for upcoming performances and links to past shows.

1535 Spruce St., 303-443-8696
etown.org/etown-hall/all-events

Boulder Falls

SPORTS
AND RECREATION

ROOT FOR THE UNIVERSITY OF COLORADO BUFFS FOOTBALL TEAM
AT FOLSOM FIELD

When the Colorado Buffaloes are playing in Boulder, parking and hotel/dinner reservations are at a premium. The night before each home game, wear black and gold to the Pearl Street Stampede. The Golden Buffalo Marching Band, the Spirit Team, and Chip (the team's mascot) march down the Pearl Street Mall and perform inside Avanti F & B. On game day, head to the official tailgate event at Ralphie's Corral for music, food, performances by the band and Spirit Team, and giveaways; or, set up your own pregame celebration in a parking lot. Arrive early to the stadium so you can witness Ralphie, a live buffalo, running with its student-athlete handlers before the start of the game. A repeat performance occurs before the start of the second half. CU football tickets can be ordered directly from the CU Buffs website.

CU-Football Game Day Guide
bouldercoloradousa.com/things-to-do/visiting-cu/cu-game-day-guide

Colorado Buffaloes Football
2150 Stadium Dr., 303-492-8337
cubuffs.com/sports/football

GLIDE ABOVE THE TREETOPS
WITH BOULDER FREE FLIGHT

From March to October, sample the sport of paragliding by taking a tandem flight at locally owned and operated Boulder Free Flight. With worldwide experience and a passion for soaring near the clouds at unique locations, Johannes Rath brought Boulder Free Flight to the area. At Foothills Community Park, participants are given safety instructions before taking their first ride. During the 5- to 35-minute flight, a GoPro records memorable moments of this thrilling experience. Your senses go into high gear as your body becomes attuned to the lifting air currents and the incredible views of the Front Range and Boulder Valley. Individuals hooked on having a bird's eye view of the world can enroll in 15 to 20 three-hour sessions to become solo paragliding pilots. In the off-season, Johannes leads international paragliding tours.

501 Locust Ave., 720-705-2505
boulderfreeflight.com

ZOOM
THROUGH BOULDER
WITH A GUIDED BICYCLE TOUR

With more than 300-miles of bike lanes and paths, Boulder has a plethora of bicycle-tour options. Guided tours are on paved, flat surfaces as well as steep, unpaved terrain. Make sure you match your comfort level, experience, and stamina with the selected itinerary. The ability to ride a bicycle is a prerequisite for all tours. E-Bike tours include a short introduction to the technology and safety. Boulder Bike Tours, Pedego, Boulder Tour Company, and Full Cycle Bikes and Colorado Multisport offer guided e-bike tours. Without breaking a sweat, it is possible to effortlessly climb steep hills to witness stunning views. After more than 50 years of living in Boulder, Herschel Goldberg, owner of Boulder Bike Tours, offers morsels of information during his mountain bike and bike-to-farm tours.

Boulder Bike Tours
info@boulderbiketours.com
303-747-6191
boulderbiketours.com/all-tours

Boulder Tour Company—Electric
Cruiser Bike Tour
700 Dellwood Ave., 720-724-8080
bouldertourcompany.com

Pedego Electric Bikes Boulder
2512 Broadway St., 303-415-9999
pedegoelectricbikes.com

Full Cycle Bikes
and Colorado Multisport
2355 30th St., 303-440-1002
fullcyclebikes.com/about/
rent-bikes-and-gear-pg115.htm

TURN OUT FOR THE UNIVERSITY OF COLORADO BUFFS BASKETBALL AND VOLLEYBALL TEAMS
AT THE CU EVENT CENTER

With more than 11,000 seats, the CU Event Center hosts men's and women's basketball and women's volleyball games as well as conferences, conventions, concerts, and trade shows. Crowd sizes fluctuate for CU men's basketball games from one season to the next. The bleachers in the upper rows are less expensive seating options, while more comfortable chairs with seat backs demand a higher price point and offer better viewing. If you forget your black and gold gear, onsite kiosks offer trendy CU Buffs apparel and souvenirs. Highly nationally ranked and Pac-12 teams garner the biggest turnouts. Nearby free parking offers convenient access but can fill up fast when playing rivals and stiffer competition. Once inside, the Buff Basketball Band, along with the cheer team, the dance team, and the costumed mascot (nicknamed Chip) keep the college spirit alive. Go Buffs!

950 Regent Dr., 303-492-8337
cubuffs.com/sports/mens-basketball

EXPLORE
ELDORADO CANYON STATE PARK

From sunrise to sunset, Eldorado Canyon State Park hikers and climbers can walk on easy to difficult unpaved hiking trails and access 500 technical rock-climbing routes on Eldo's golden cliffs. The moderate-level Rattlesnake Gulch Trail passes by the ruins of the early 20th-century Crags Hotel and includes multiple photo opportunities. From the shorter and easier Fowler Trail, you can stand in awe while watching accomplished rock climbers scale the 700-foot-high sandstone cliffs. Climbers assume the inherent risk of this dangerous sport. More sedentary folks can simply gaze at the rocky terrain or fish in the South Boulder Creek for rainbow, brook, and brown trout, longnose dace, and white and longnose suckers. Parking can be problematic during peak summer months, so consider an early start.

9 Kneale Rd., Eldorado Springs, 303-494-3943
cpw.state.co.us/placestogo/parks/eldoradocanyon

SWIM, BOAT, OR HIKE
AT THE BOULDER RESERVOIR

Inland mountain communities rarely offer a beach experience. Boulder is fortunate to have the Boulder Reservoir (or "the Rez") to satisfy your desire to engage in aquatic sports. Seasonal changes offer different opportunities. Warmer temperatures attract swimmers and sunbathers who embrace the opportunity to swim and relax with a foothill backdrop. Other options include learning how to sail or renting a stand-up paddleboard or pontoon boat. A variety of fish can be caught after purchasing a Colorado Parks and Wildlife fishing license. Pedestrians, bikers, and runners can follow the 5.3-mile Boulder Reservoir Loop and take time to enjoy a picnic before departing. In season, take a beverage or snack break at the Driftwind at the Rez. A bonus to visiting off-season is free admission and the option to bring a dog.

Boulder Reservoir
5275 Reservoir Rd., 303-441-3461
bouldercolorado.gov/locations/boulder-reservoir

Driftwind at the Rez
5565 51 St., manager@driftwindboulder.com
driftwindboulder.com

Rocky Mountain Paddleboard
info@rockymtnpaddleboard.com, 720-943-1132
rockymtnpaddleboard.com

SAIL THROUGH THE AIR
ON A BALLOON TOUR

An early morning hot air balloon ride at 1,000 to 3,000 feet above the ground reveals a stunning, panoramic view of Boulder Valley. Local temperature and wind conditions mandate early-morning launches from May to mid-November. Everyone from older children to senior citizens can enjoy this peaceful ride. Packages vary from company to company. Starting decades ago, Life Cycle Balloons began conducting commercial rides focusing on intimate adventures limited to four people. To avoid Boulder's unpredictable winds, the company launches in S.E. Longmont and has a secondary site in South Park, 55 miles west of Colorado Springs. Fair Winds Hot Air Balloon Flights and its subcontractor Aero-Cruise Balloon Adventures take off from open space in Erie with balloons accommodating two to 14 passengers. Ideal times are late spring and autumn.

Lifecycle Balloon Adventures
303-216-1900
lifecycleballoons.com

Aero-Cruise Balloon Adventures
890 Hemlock Way, Broomfield, 303-469-1243
aerocruiseballoonadventures.com

Fair Winds Hot Air Balloon Flights
2140 N 107th St., Lafayette, 303-939-9323
hotairballoonridescolorado.com

EMBRACE MOTHER NATURE
WITH A COLORADO WILDERNESS RIDES AND GUIDES TOUR

Adventure seekers who want to maximize their time exploring and learning about Colorado's natural resources can easily become overwhelmed with the multitude of available activities. Colorado Wilderness Rides and Guides is a full-service tour operator specializing in seasonal guided outdoor activities for all ability levels, including hiking, backpacking, rock climbing, mountaineering, bike tours, fishing, float trips, white water rafting, ziplining, snowshoeing, and skiing. They also book general sightseeing tours for people of all ages. Joshua Baruch and his team offer half-day, full-day, and multiple-day packages and are open to designing custom packages to fulfill the specific requests of individuals, couples, and families who want to learn a new skill or become actively engaged in numerous adventures near Boulder and Rocky Mountain National Park.

6560 Odell Pl., 720-242-9828
coloradowildernessridesandguides.com

BE TRANSPORTED THROUGH BOULDER
ON A COLORADO SEGWAY

Instead of exploring Boulder by walking, riding a bicycle, or driving a car, hop on a Segway. The 90-minute tour starts in the historic Whittier neighborhood, heads west to Chautauqua, and then winds back through the Pearl Street Mall before returning to the starting point. Participants need to be at least 14 years old, weigh between 100 and 260 pounds, exhibit balance, and have the stamina to stand for at least 45 minutes. A 30-minute training session is given before each departure. During the journey, the small group will pause about a dozen times to learn morsels of information about Boulder's history and culture. Rides can be personalized to include special routes and stops. Colorado Segway Tours also operates in Denver.

20th Street and Mapleton Avenue, 303-449-6780
coloradosegwaytours.com/segway-tours/boulder-segway-tour

LEARN MOUNTAIN SPORTS AND SAFETY
WITH A COLORADO MOUNTAIN SCHOOL PROFESSIONAL GUIDE

Colorado Mountain School, accredited by the American Guides Association and recognized by the American Institute for Avalanche Research (AIARE) as the country's #1 avalanche-course provider, offers year-round classes for ice climbing, rock climbing, backcountry skiing, and avalanche training. From May to October, families participate in the Half Day Fun Climb in Estes Park, while individuals seeking a more intense adventure sign up for the Intro to Rock Climbing. A custom, full-day, guided trip up the first Flatiron can be reserved for those who are game. When the days get colder and longer, backcountry skiers seeking safety are lured to the popular AIARE 1 Hybrid Course and the AIARE 1 Three Day Course. Skiers who are interested in backcountry skiing gravitate to the Intro to Backcountry Skiing and Splitskiing and the RMNP (Rocky Mountain National Park) Classic Ski Tour.

633 S Broadway St., 720-387-8944
coloradomountainschool.com

RELAX
AT THE HISTORIC
ELDORADO SPRINGS POOL

Decades before Eldorado Canyon State Park was created in 1978, the park's acreage and adjacent property were owned by the Fowler Family, who ran the Eldorado Springs Resort until 1983. When the resort, nicknamed the "Coney Island of the West," opened in 1905, visitors came by horseback and train to relax and take a dip in the resort's pool. The resort was associated with the natural artesian spring water originating from rain and snow just east of the Continental Divide and then filtered through a natural process. Notable guests included Dwight and Mamie Eisenhower, W. C. Fields, and Jack Dempsey, as well as many other celebrities. After updates are completed to the roadway, swimming pool, bathrooms, and amenities, the pool will reopen in the summer of 2023.

294 Artesian Dr., 303-604-3000
eldoradosprings.com/swimming-pool

FISH
WITH FRONT RANGE ANGLERS

Unlike other places where fishing is a seasonal sport, Coloradoans can fish year-round. Moderate temperatures in the Front Range make it possible to fish throughout the winter. Two types of customers enter the Front Range Anglers shop on Pearl Street. Some are looking to purchase equipment and to learn as much as they can about fly fishing and the best places to go fishing, while others have already booked one of the 100 trips offered annually. Most people select the store's signature trip to Rocky Mountain National Park, which has two options: a half day and a full day. If you prefer to fish locally, you will be in for a surprise. The brown trout were born in Boulder Creek and were not imported from another source.

2344 Pearl St., 303-494-1375
frontrangeanglers.com/guided-trips

TAKE A
PADDLEBOARD LESSON
WITH ROCKY MOUNTAIN PADDLEBOARD

A trip to the Boulder Reservoir is incomplete without a watersport experience. After spending summers in Boulder, Shawn Rodine recognized the need for watersport equipment at the reservoir. In a land-locked state with limited watersports, Rocky Mountain Paddleboard introduces novices to paddleboarding and provides intermediate lessons for those who understand the basics. Thousands of people have taken advantage of the convenience of renting paddleboards, kayaks, canoes, and pedal boats. Many come for the company's popular events—full-moon paddles, sunset eco-tours, and river clinics. Instructors inspire others to embrace challenges and find the peace and serenity that can only be found on the water. Rocky Mountain Paddleboard is also located at the Union Reservoir in Longmont, Bear Creek Lake Park in Lakewood, and the Cherry Creek Reservoir in Denver.

info@rockymtnpaddleboard.com, 720-943-1132
rockymtnpaddleboard.com

UNCOVER
BOULDER'S STREET ART
WITH A SELF-GUIDED MURAL VIEWING

Outdoor murals capture the essence of a city. By car, bike, or foot, one can follow the routes depicted on self-guided-tour maps. Online sites offer a deeper understanding of these outdoor art treasures. Since the inception of the Street Wise Boulder project in 2019, new creations by local, national, and international artists are added during the annual ARTivism mural festival. Vibrant color combinations highlight the artists' messages, which focus on an assortment of social issues and cultures. The topics range from the pandemic to preserving the environment to the plights of a variety of different groups. Boulder's diverse art scene can be enjoyed in conjunction with visits to the historic business area or other neighborhoods throughout Boulder. If you prefer a guided bicycle tour, consider JD's Joyrides.

Street Wise Arts Boulder
streetwiseboulder.com

JD's Joyrides
2030 17th St., 303-818-5280
jdsjoyrides.com

EXPLORE
THE BOULDER CREEK PATH

From 55th Street in East Boulder to an endpoint in Boulder Canyon, pedestrians, joggers, and bikers weave their way through green space, the university campus, and the downtown area on a mostly paved trail running along a rocky creek bed. On Wednesdays and Saturdays, take a detour to the Boulder Farmers Market (13th Street between Canyon and Arapahoe) to sample a local treat. Take a break by picnicking at an adjacent park. Consider Eben G. Fine Park, Central Park, or Scott Carpenter Park. Water lovers can satisfy their adventurous spirits by renting tubes and kayaks at nearby venues, while licensed individuals can try their luck at fly fishing. Before launching from the creek's shoreline, remember to check for safe water levels.

Boulder Creek Path
alltrails.com/trail/us/colorado/
boulder-creek-path

Front Range Anglers
2344 Pearl St., 303-494-1375
frontrangeanglers.com/guided-trips

Whitewater Tubing & Recreation
2709 Spruce St., 720-239-2179
whitewatertubing.com

Rocky Mountain Anglers
1904 Arapahoe Ave., 303-447-2400
rockymtanglers.com

Boulder Farmers Market
13th Street between Canyon Drive and Arapahoe Avenue, 303-910-2236
bcfm.org

SHOOT PHOTOS
AT BOULDER FALLS

You can drive 11 miles (approximately 20 minutes) from downtown Boulder to witness a 70-foot waterfall surrounded by narrow canyon cliffs lined with ponderosa pines. Boulder Falls has been a popular attraction for many generations. Restorations have improved the safety and access to this must-see spot. The short (0.3-mile) trail can be combined with a day trip to Nederland. Other options are to hike the lengthy and moderately difficult Devil's Thumb Pass Trail near Nederland, the easier 3-mile Forsythe Canyon Trail to a potential dried-up waterfall and reservoir, or the steep and strenuous 3.2-mile Mount Sanitas Trail, revealing amazing views of Boulder. The Mount Sanitas trailhead has a few easier options. It is wise to visit the Boulder Falls and trailhead websites to check for winter-month and periodic closures.

bouldercolorado.gov/trail/boulder-falls

MEANDER
ON A LOCAL TRAIL

When you come from sea level, you may not be ready to tackle Boulder's challenging trails. At an altitude of approximately 5,400 feet, it is possible to feel the effects of less oxygen: headache, nausea, and fatigue. Without getting out of breath, one can easily enjoy Colorado sunshine and easier terrain with a chance of seeing wildlife. Plan your outing by reviewing an online trail map to determine the length, difficulty level, and terrain of the path. Some trailheads can be accessed by foot or by public transportation, while others require a car. Popular trails will be more crowded on weekends and holidays. Remember to pack sufficient water to avoid dehydration. Some parking lots have fees. Watch for signs for parking rules.

bouldercolorado.gov/government/departments/open-space-mountain-parks

alltrails.com/us/colorado/boulder

TIP

To avoid being disappointed, check for closures.

SUGGESTED EASIER TRAILS

Boy Scout Trail near Flagstaff Nature Center

Flatirons Vista south of Boulder along
Highway 93

Anne U. White Trail near Fourmile
Canyon Creek

Red Rocks Trail near downtown Boulder

Sawhill Ponds Trail east Boulder
south of Gunbarrel

Wonderland Lake Loop in a
North Boulder neighborhood

HIKE
CHAUTAUQUA PARK

If you are like most people, you enter Boulder via the Boulder–Denver Turnpike, and on a clear day you might pull over at the Davidson Mesa Overlook to view the foothills. Trekkers and climbers who are drawn to the base of the Flatirons will be enticed by the selection of interconnected trails at Chautauqua Park. The Chautauqua Loop Trail and the Enchanted Mesa Trail are perfect for individuals comfortable with grassy meadows and modest inclines leading to overlooks. Experienced hikers seeking a closer look at the towering sandstone slabs can follow the First and Second Flatiron Trail and the Second and Third Flatiron Trail. For a strenuous ascent, tackle the Royal Arch Trail and the Green Mountain Loop via Chautauqua Trail.

bouldercoloradousa.com/outdoors/hiking/chautauqua-hikes

SKI LIKE A LOCAL
AT ELDORA MOUNTAIN

Avoid the traffic jams on I-70 and the hustle and bustle of a major ski area by driving 20 miles to the smaller Eldora ski area, offering more than 350 skiable acres accessed by 10 lifts with an assortment of runs—cruisers, steeps, bumps, and terrains. Cross-country skiers and snowshoers head to the Nordic Center, which hosts over 40 kilometers of trails. Woodward, an action sports company, expanded its presence to Eldora in 2018 to teach skills to skiers and riders. Onsite facilities are limited, so many visitors find their way to nearby Nederland, which has more shops and restaurants. Eldora parking lots fill up quickly, so it is advisable to arrive early, carpool with others, or take an RTD bus or shuttle from Boulder.

2861 Eldora Ski Rd., Nederland, 303-440-8700
eldora.com, nederlandco.org/things-to-do

CLIMB HIGHER
ON A CHALLENGING TRAIL

Physically fit adventure seekers who are up for a challenge should select trails identified as moderate to difficult. Trails with these designations have altitude gains covering more distance. Longer hikes require appropriate footwear and a daypack filled with water, food, bandages, raingear, a jacket, and sunscreen. Steeper trails can be taxing for those unfamiliar with mountain environments, so focusing on where you are stepping is essential. It is easy to get lost if you step off the path. Be prepared for dangerous wildlife—bears, mountain lions, snakes, and other creatures. Weather conditions can change abruptly in the foothills near Boulder. Avoid a dangerous situation by not taking unnecessary risks. If possible, don't go solo. Check online for information about closures, trail conditions, and parking fees.

bouldercolorado.gov/government/departments/open-space-mountain-parks

alltrails.com/us/colorado/boulder

TRAILS TO SCALE
Bear Peak
Mesa Trail
Chapman Drive and Tenderfoot Trail on Flagstaff Mountain
Mount Sanitas Trailhead on Mapleton Avenue west of 4th
South Boulder Peak
Green Mountain Summit Loop

COMPETE
IN AN ANNUAL ATHLETIC EVENT

World-class athletes along with amateur participants are drawn to Boulder. Some come to train, while others come to compete. For decades, Boulder has sponsored the BolderBoulder running event during Memorial Day weekend. Its popularity has grown significantly, with more than 50,000 runners participating in the last few races. More than a million people have crossed the finish line since the first competition in 1979. Boulder's foothill location provides an ideal spot for the summer Ironman 70.3 triathlon. Participants swim in the Boulder Reservoir, bike on the rolling hills of Boulder County, and run 13.1 miles near the reservoir. During the annual Buffalo Bicycle Classic, sponsored by Elevations Credit Union, money is raised for CU scholarships for students demonstrating significant financial need.

Bolderboulder 10K Road Race
5720 Flatiron Pkwy., 303-444-RACE
bolderboulder.com

Ironman 70.3 Boulder
1795 Dogwood St., Ste. 300, 717-421-4121
ironman.com/im703-boulder

Buffalo Bicycle Classic
275 UCB, 303-735-1569
colorado.edu/event/buffalobicycleclassic

GO BIRDWATCHING
WITH A GUIDED HIKE

Connect with the Boulder County Audubon Society, the Front Range Birding Company, the City of Boulder, and Boulder County websites to learn more about Boulder's amazing wildlife. Since the 1970s, the Boulder County Audubon Society has offered field trips focusing on local birds and wildlife on Boulder Open Space and Mountain Park trails. The other groups offer similar events. Avid birdwatchers and novices can easily join a free program. On your own, check out Sawhill and Walden Ponds Wildlife Areas, Teller Farms, South Boulder Creek Trail at Bobolink Trailhead, the Boulder Reservoir, and Wonder Lake. A short car ride south will take you to Dowdy Draw Trail, the South Mesa Trail, and Eldorado Canyon State Park. Meyers Gulch Trail at Walker Ranch is a mountain favorite.

Boulder County Audubon Society
boulderaudubon.org/all-events?category=field%20trips

Front Range Birding Company
frontrangebirding.com/community

City of Boulder Nature Hikes and Programs
bouldercolorado.gov/services/nature-hikes-and-programs

Boulder County Hikes and Events
bouldercounty.org/open-space/activities/calendar

CAMP IN A YURT
AT GOLDEN GATE CANYON STATE PARK

Yurts offer an escape from urban lifestyles. These round tents on wooden frames can be rented at Golden Gate Canyon State Park, about 30 minutes from Boulder. Each yurt can accommodate six people. The rustic accommodations at the park include outdoor campfire rings and nearby restrooms/showers, but no refrigeration. While hiking on the 12 year-round park trails, be aware that the park does not have cell phone or internet service. The easily accessible and well-maintained trails are shared in the summer by hikers, mountain bikers, and horseback riders; and in the winter months by cross-country skiers and snowshoers. Be on the lookout for moose, bears, mule deer, and elk as well as smaller mammals like foxes, porcupines, beavers, and coyotes. Summer programming includes campfire events and kid-friendly programs.

92 Crawford Gulch Rd., Golden, 303-582-3707
cpw.state.co.us/placestogo/parks/goldengatecanyon

VISIT RESCUED ANIMALS
AT THE WILD ANIMAL SANCTUARY

When hiking near Boulder your likelihood of seeing native wildlife is uncertain. To satisfy your wildlife interest, take an hour's drive to visit the Wild Animal Sanctuary. This facility works with state, national, and international government agencies to provide safe havens for rescued animals and handle overflow from overcrowded zoos. Rescued animals need a habitat where they can move without restraints in a natural environment. At the Welcome Center guests learn more about the nation's captive wildlife crisis and the sanctuary's response. The Mile into the Wild Walkway, an elevated one-and-a-half-mile pathway with observation platforms, provides access to the site and protects visitors from the tigers, wolves, bears, leopards, hyenas, lions, bobcats, lynx, foxes, camels, yaks, alpacas, and other animals who live in the sanctuary. Set aside several hours for this adventure.

2999 County Rd. 53, Keenesburg, 303-536-0118
wildanimalsanctuary.org

DRIVE UP
FLAGSTAFF MOUNTAIN

If switchback turns on a mountain road are within your comfort zone, take Baseline Road west to Flagstaff Road. As the road winds its way up Flagstaff Mountain, you will either love or hate the hairpin-turn experience with limited guard rails. While hearty souls prefer to spend the day hiking the steep paths, many find the car journey to be a spectacular way to get panoramic views of Boulder and to reach the Sunrise Amphitheater, a popular wedding venue, without breaking a sweat. Several other historical structures can be reached from the road, as can the Flagstaff Nature Center and the Flagstaff House Restaurant, a popular fine-dining venue. Multiple pull-off points with paid parking provide access to the trail system.

bouldercolorado.gov/trail/flagstaff

WITNESS ELK BUGLING
IN ROCKY MOUNTAIN NATIONAL PARK

Rocky Mountain National Park is one of four national parks in Colorado. This massive park of more than 400 square miles lies between Estes Park and Grand Lake, with 60 mountain peaks over 12,000 feet above sea level and 156 lakes. The main draws from Memorial Day to late autumn are Trail Ridge Road and 355 miles of hiking trails. During this time period, horseback riders can sign up for scheduled rides offered by Hi Country Stables/Glacier Creek Stables, National Park Gateway Stables, and Jackson Stables. Early summer wildflowers add color to the spectacular terrain, and from mid-September to mid-October significant crowds gather to witness large numbers of elk bugling during their mating season. The bulls use a series of sounds to communicate to the other elk in the herd. Many spectators stand for hours admiring this annual ritual. Before heading out for the day, check for road closures.

4600 Fall River Rd., Estes Park, 970-586-1206
nps.gov/romo/planyourvisit/basicinfo.htm

TIP
To control access to the national park, the National Park Service sometimes requires a timed-entry reservation. Check the website to determine if reservations are required.

Hi Country Stables/Glacier Creek Stables
970-444-2716
rockymountainhorserides.com

National Park Gateway Stables
970-586-5269
skhorses.com/national-park-gateway-stables

Jackson Stables
970-586-3341
jacksonstables.com

APPRECIATE YOUR SURROUNDINGS
ON A MILE-HIGH GLIDING SAILPLANE

Are you receptive to being 3,000 to 7,000 feet above the ground in a glider? Mile High Gliding offers year-round adventures with heated cockpits. Only rain, snow, and winds over 10 knots cause flight delays. Without distracting motor sounds, the ride is peaceful and serene. Many passengers are content to absorb the amazing views of Boulder Valley and the foothills. More daring participants take part in crazier rides with spirals, steep turns, and unpredictable rises and falls. The 35-minute Mile High Flight is the most popular option. On this route, people get a bird's-eye view of the Continental Divide, Nederland, Gold Hill, downtown Boulder, the university, and other area landmarks. The combined weight of two passengers cannot exceed 300 pounds.

5534 Independence Rd., 303-527-1122
milehighgliding.com

STARE INTO THE EVENING SKY
WITH AN ELEVATED ASTRONOMY TOUR

Take advantage of cloudless Boulder nights by signing up for an Elevated Astronomy tour. Beginning at sundown, stargazers and novices gather at a designated spot at the Boulder Valley Ranch for an engaging two-hour experience. Sitting on a camp seat, participants munch on snacks and listen to an informative introductory talk focusing on the planets, constellations, navigation satellites, nebulae, shooting stars, and the universe mixed with a bit of folklore. Rookie stargazers will learn the ins and outs of using a telescope and how to identify celestial objects. This is a great opportunity for school-aged children to learn about the universe in a low-key setting. Similar tours are also available in Winter Park. Falling evening temperatures may call for a jacket.

luke@astrotours.org, 303-324-5831
astrotours.org

SPEND A DAY
AT A WORLD-CLASS SKI RESORT

Skiers and boarders will find it hard to resist a day at a world-class Colorado ski resort. Enjoying this experience will require an early morning start and the willingness to potentially sit in a traffic jam on I-70. Winter Park, Loveland, Keystone Resort, Breckenridge, Copper Mountain, Arapahoe Basin, and Vail can be reached in less than two hours when snow conditions and accidents do not cause delays. Snow conditions fluctuate from season to season, but the ideal time to visit is from December through March. Amenities at Loveland and Arapahoe Basin are minimal, while Breckenridge, Winter Park, and Vail are enhanced by an adjacent town. Copper Mountain has wonderful ski conditions but limited dining options and stores. Keystone Resort is has more skiable terrain and offers a greater selection of restaurants. Additional dining options are located in nearby Dillon, Frisco, and Silverthorne. Dehydration is a major concern, so don't forget to bring water for the long day.

Colorado Ski Country USA
3773 Cherry Creek N Dr., Denver, 303-837-0793
coloradoski.com

Genesee Mountain Park
720-865-0900
denvergov.org/content/denvergov/en/denver-parks-and-recreation/parks/
mountain-parks/genesee-mountain-park.html

TIP

On the way back from the mountains, consider a short stop at Genesee Park. Heading eastbound on I-70, get off at Exit 254 to view a herd of bison and to take pictures of the Continental Divide. Check the website to find the location of the three pastures. Another option is to eat dinner in Golden, an historic town at the base of the foothills. Notable attractions include the Coors Brewery Tour, Buffalo Bill's Museum and Grave, Boettcher Mansion, and the Colorado Railroad Museum.

visitgolden.com

Inside Hotel Boulderado

CULTURE AND HISTORY

GO BACK IN TIME
WITH A HOTEL BOULDERADO TOUR

Touring this iconic landmark takes you back to the beginning of the 20th century, when Boulder was a community of approximately 6,000 residents. Stockholders banded together to create "the community's hotel." Back then, the entrance was on Spruce Street instead of 13th Street, and the daily room rate was between $1 and $2.50. Guests came with trunks and often stayed for a month. During a tour, in-house historian Lauren McKown intersperses local history with photographs and snippets about the original furnishings. History lovers will ooh and ahh at the mixture of Spanish Revival and Italian Renaissance details, combined with solid cherry woodwork and the multistory lobby staircase, a popular site for many weddings. Numerous renovations have maintained the property without destroying its architectural charm.

2115 13th St., 303-442-4344
boulderado.com/history-tours

BE INTRODUCED TO BOULDER'S CULTURE
WITH A LOCAL TABLE TOUR

Food is often the entry point to understanding a city's culture. Foodies participating in one of Megan Bucholz's Taste of Boulder tours visit five locations in Boulder's historic downtown. Individuals need to walk from place to place in varying weather conditions. The appetizer, entrée, and dessert samplings along with complimentary beverages reveal the dynamic nature of Boulder's eclectic food scene, which features authentic ethnic dishes, American favorites, and signature alcoholic beverages. After partnering with dozens of locally owned food vendors, including a spice shop, Megan can offer a unique culinary experience week after week with varying portion sizes. If given advance notice, she will accommodate most dietary requests. Along the route, Megan points out historical sites and shares information about Boulder's culture. She also runs similar food tours in both Fort Collins and Denver.

303-909-5747
localtabletours.com

ATTEND
A NATIONAL CENTER FOR ATMOSPHERIC RESEARCH (NCAR) GUIDED TOUR

When you drive into Boulder it is impossible to miss NCAR's towering buildings. These architectural gems, designed by world-renowned Chinese architect I. M. Pei, are strategically placed on a prominent mesa at the base of the Flatirons. Stone from nearby quarries was used to create these striking structures modeled after the Native American dwellings in Colorado's Mesa Verde National Park. This premier foothill location is also a notable access point for many spectacular hiking trails. Since 1960, NCAR's award-winning scientists have collaborated with the worldwide scientific community. Guided and self-guided tours showcase some of NCAR's accomplishments. Colorful interactive displays demonstrate the connection between the Earth and its atmosphere. The informative tours are suitable for adults and school-aged children. Another visitor center is in Cheyenne, Wyoming.

1850 Table Mesa Dr., 303-497-2401
scied.ucar.edu/visit/ncar-public-tours

VIEW CUTTING-EDGE ART
AT BOULDER MUSEUM
OF CONTEMPORARY ART (BMoCA)

During a visit to the Pearl Street Mall or before stopping at the Boulder Farmers Market, lovers of abstract modern art can take a detour to the BMoCA. Upon entering a vintage early 20th-century former red brick warehouse on 13th Street, you can escape from everyday concerns. Stroll through the curated exhibits presented in a handful of intimate galleries. Some exhibits may inspire reflection, while others will simply be admired. Past exhibits showcased an impressive list of local, national, and international artists representing a wide range of artistic expression. A rotating list of mostly seasonal exhibits is shared online. In-person programs for adults, for people suffering from Alzheimer's and dementia, and for children occur monthly to inspire interest in the arts.

1750 13th St., 303-443-2122
bmoca.org

ENCOUNTER DIVERSE ARTISTIC EXPRESSION
AT THE CU ART MUSEUM

Take advantage of the free admission to this CU museum found in the Visual Arts Complex. The exhibitions and programs spotlight diverse cultures and communities covering 10,000 years of history. Visitors are inspired by an array of perspectives and the depth of the holdings. The Ancient and Classical Collection features rare coins from the Roman Empire. Greek, Roman, and Chinese vessels are also part of the museum's inventory. Other artwork focuses on contemporary drawings, paintings, printmaking, woodcuts, ceramics, photographs, and digital media. A weekly Friday workshop combines an exploration of art with a mindful practice. The public is invited to lectures, gallery talks, concerts, performances, and workshops. Parking can be challenging near the campus. The closest parking is at the Euclid Autopark at the corner of Euclid Avenue and 18th Street.

1085 18th St., 303-492-8300
colorado.edu/cuartmuseum

LEARN ABOUT BOULDER'S PAST
AT THE MUSEUM OF BOULDER
AT TEBO CENTER

It is no surprise that a university town would generate an abundance of cultural and scientific accomplishments. The museum's permanent exhibit, the Boulder Experience Gallery, captures the essence of Boulder's influence on Colorado and the rest of the world. Through state-of-the-art hands-on and multi-media exhibits, visitors are introduced to the Southern Arapahoe tribe. These indigenous people were severely impacted by the Pikes Peak Gold Rush settlers who arrived in Boulder Valley in 1858. Moving forward in time, the displays highlight the contributions to human achievement residents of Boulder have made in the 20th and 21st centuries. Younger children gravitate to the Playzeum, where they can engage in an imaginative and innovate play environment. Children over the age of five can build their own robots in the Google Garage. Temporary exhibits appear throughout the year.

2205 Broadway St., 303-449-3464
museumofboulder.org

DELVE INTO COLORADO, NORTH AMERICAN, AND WORLD HISTORY
AT THE MUSEUM OF NATURAL HISTORY

It isn't an everyday occurrence at a Boulder home to unearth more than 80 stone tools dating to approximately 13,000 years ago. During the process of landscaping Patrick Mahaffy's home in 2008, this unique assortment of tools was discovered. This must-see collection is housed in the Unearthed: Ancient Life in the Boulder Valley exhibit in Anthropology Hall. The informative displays explain the significance of this rare find. Many do not realize that Colorado is known as one of the richest fossil regions in North America. The permanent exhibit, Fossils: Clues to the Past, engages young and old by showing how ancient plants and animals offer clues to Earth's history. Even though this exhibit is small, it includes animals from just thousands of years ago to ancient organisms from hundreds of millions of years ago. Guided programs and hands-on workshops offer a more comprehensive experience.

Henderson Building, 15th Street and Broadway, 303-492-6892
colorado.edu/cumuseum

WALK THROUGH
THE SHELBY AMERICAN
COLLECTION MUSEUM

In a quiet industrial park in North Boulder you can enter an unassuming warehouse to see approximately 40 Shelby race cars built in the 1960s along with photographs and an abundance of car-racing memorabilia. In addition, you can watch an informative video. Back in 1996, the museum's collection started with just eight cars. Today, car lovers, history buffs, and museum visitors can see firsthand how Carroll Hall Shelby (1923–2012) changed race-car history. As an international race-car driver, he drove the fastest European cars available. In 1959, he was the winner of the 24 Hours of Le Mans. To compete head to head with the European race-car industry, Shelby founded Shelby American and produced the Cobra, Shelby Mustang, and Ford GT40 cars. Onsite posters reveal the incredible success of Shelby American's legendary cars.

5020 Chaparral Ct., 303-516-9565
shelbyamericancollection.org

DISCOVER THE HISTORY OF THE UNIVERSITY OF COLORADO
WITH A SELF-GUIDED TOUR

CU Boulder is frequently cited as one of the most beautiful American campuses. The signature sandstone walls with red tile roofs buildings sit at the base of the Flatirons and the distant Rocky Mountains. Start at Old Main, where the campus began. Inside, you can trace CU's history at the Heritage Center. Next, head to the Mary Rippon Outdoor Theater (1936), home of the Colorado Shakespeare Festival. Other notable landmarks are the Henderson Building (1937), the Museum of Natural History; and Macky Auditorium (1921), a performance facility for concerts, the CU Artist Series, and the Boulder Philharmonic Orchestra. If time allows, visit Norlin Library, Folsom Field (the home of the CU football team), the Visual Arts Complex (CU Art Museum), and Fiske Planetarium.

Heritage Center
1600 Pleasant St., 303-492-6329
colorado.edu/alumni/stories/heritagecenter

campusvisitorguides.com/cu/self-guided-tour

bouldercoloradousa.com/things-to-do/experiences-and-tours/self-guided-tours

PARTICIPATE IN THE CONFERENCE
ON WORLD AFFAIRS WEEK AND THE YEAR-ROUND SPEAKER SERIES

College campuses are centers of discussion and debate. The Conference on World Affairs maintains a dialogue throughout the year. It promotes a year-round Speaker Series that brings panelists from all over the worlds to exchange ideas with the goal of engaging, educating, and inspiring the university community, the local community, and even a worldwide audience. For decades, the Conference on World Affairs has set aside four days in April to bring together approximately 100 speakers and performers from around the world to discuss pertinent issues. In 2022, the conference resumed its in-person events and offered a selection of livestreamed online sessions. A jazz concert is held in conjunction with the weeklong event. The Speaker Series and the weeklong conference are free and open to the public.

1344 Grandview Ave., 303-492-2525
colorado.edu/cwa

VISIT
THE COLORADO CHAUTAUQUA
NATIONAL HISTORIC LANDMARK

Chautauqua is Boulder's top comprehensive outdoor venue. As one of Colorado's 26 National Historic Landmarks, it is the only western Chautauqua facility with operational original structures. By reserving a cottage at the base of the Flatirons, guests can access 40 miles of adjacent hiking trails and tour the city. Stop in at the Ranger Cottage or access the online trail map before heading out. Throughout the day, guests can dine in the 19th-century Chautauqua Dining Hall and purchase snacks and supplies at the General Store. For more than a century, people have attended film festivals, musical concerts, dance performances, educational programs, and presentations by notable speakers in the Chautauqua Auditorium and Community House. With limited parking, consider taking the park-to-park shuttle on summer weekends.

900 Baseline Rd., 303-442-3282
chautauqua.com

STROLL THROUGH BOULDER'S HISTORIC NEIGHBORHOODS—
MAPLETON HILL, WHITTIER, AND UNIVERSITY HILL

Even though cabins from the gold rush no longer exist, it is possible to take a self-guided walking tour to look at homes built at the end of the 19th century and beginning of the 20th century. Boulder at that time had three established neighborhoods— Whittier, Mapleton, and University Hill. Visit Pine Street in the Whittier neighborhood to view large architect-designed homes. In the Mapleton Hill Historic District, 57 percent of the homes were built before 1910 and are enhanced by the 200 mature trees planted in the late 19th century. While some of the rock and brick homes were built around the time of the opening of Chautauqua, most existing University Hill homes were constructed in the 1920s and 1930s, when several revival styles were in vogue. In Boulder's most architecturally diverse neighborhood, individuals can see examples of Gothic and Colonial revival along with bungalows and buildings influenced by Mediterranean and Victorian styles.

bouldercoloradousa.com/things-to-do/
experiences-and-tours/self-guided-tours

● ●

GAMBLE AND RECALL HISTORY
AT BLACKHAWK AND CENTRAL CITY

Casinos are the main attraction in these former Pikes Peak Gold Rush towns approximately an hour from Boulder. When you are not gambling in the summer months, check out the Gilpin History Museum, the Gilpin County Arts Association, the Teller House, the Thomas House, the Coeur D'Alene Mine Shaft House tour, or the Hidee Gold Mine tour, or head to the Apex and Nevadaville ghost towns. The fifth-oldest professional opera house in the US, the Central City Opera House hosts a summer festival from July through August. If you don't mind driving, take the Peak-to-Peak Byway, a 55-mile scenic byway running from Black Hawk to Nederland and finishing near Estes Park, or book a horseback tour with A & A Historical Trail Ride with amazing views and morsels of local history.

Gilpin Historical Society
200 E High St., Central City, 303-582-5283
gilpinhistory.org

A & A Historical Trail Ride
188 Alps Hill Rd., Central City, 303-567-4808
aastables.com

RESERVE A SPOT
FOR A NOAA GUIDED TOUR

National Oceanic and Atmospheric Administration (NOAA) scientists predict changes in the climate, weather, ocean, and coasts and work to preserve and manage coastal and marine ecosystems and resources. An engaging, 90-minute guided tour introduces visitors to the Boulder location for this federal agency. Guests are escorted to four distinct areas—the Space Weather Prediction Center, the Global Monitoring Laboratory, the National Weather Service, and Science on a Sphere Theater. In two rooms, a glass partition separates the tour from the scientists. Participants can watch scientists in real time monitoring data on numerous computer screens. It is hard not to be impressed by the last room, where the focal point is a six-foot diameter interactive globe using real-time images of Earth. The guide points out an assortment of atmospheric and climate events.

325 Broadway St., noaa.dsrc.tours@noaa.gov
esrl.noaa.gov

BECOME INSPIRED
AT FISKE PLANETARIUM

Boulder enjoys more than 300 days of sunshine each year, so inclement weather conditions rarely cause people to seek indoor attractions. While the Fiske Planetarium on the CU Campus is an excellent choice on those days, adults and children are mesmerized year round by the spectacular shows displayed on a 65-foot-diameter dome, the largest planetarium between Chicago and Los Angeles. Weekend matinees are designed to inspire school-aged children to become interested in science. The Saturday and Sunday schedule often includes back-to-back programs. The evening shows dazzle the senses with spectacular, cutting-edge productions made possible by an 8K Sky-Skan projection system. Check the website for the upcoming schedule of full-dome films and star shows, laser fantasy and liquid sky music shows, musical concerts, and live talks by prominent scientists.

2414 Regent Dr., 303-492-5002
colorado.edu/fiske

Fiske Planetarium Projection

Pearl Street Mall

SHOPPING AND FASHION

EMBRACE THE HEART
OF DOWNTOWN BOULDER:
VISIT PEARL STREET MALL

Restaurants, shops, and street performers line this pedestrian-only walkway. Decades ago, four blocks of Boulder's historic downtown area (between 11th and 15th Streets) were transformed into a marketplace extending a few blocks east and west from the mall area and spilling over into adjacent streets and alleyways. Clothing, sporting goods, and souvenirs are available at retail outlets selling mass-produced items. More discriminating shoppers can admire handcrafted jewelry, stroll through art galleries, search for gifts, pick out one-of-a-kind merchandise made in Boulder, or select heirloom pieces from an antique shop. Year round, you can sip hot or cold beverages at local cafés and bars, snack on healthy entrées, or dine at award-winning restaurants. The Tulip Fairy and Elf Festival introduces the spring season. Summer brings live musical performances along with the Pearl Street Arts Fest. After school starts, people congregate for the Downtown Boulder Fall Fest and the Munchkin Masquerade. Light Up the Holidays events end the year.

Downtown Boulder
1942 Broadway St., 303-449-3774
boulderdowntown.com

TIP

Parking is free on Sundays and holidays. At other times, if you are willing to walk a few blocks, there are nearby streets offering free parking.

IMMERSE YOURSELF IN COLLEGE CULTURE
BY VISITING UNIVERSITY HILL (OR "THE HILL")

Students, locals, and visitors head to The Hill, directly west of CU, to shop, dine at hangouts, and be entertained. This commercial area is surrounded by hilly streets lined with fraternities, sororities, and vintage homes, some dating back to the end of the 19th century and the early part of the 20th century. While not all landmarks have survived, Fox Theatre has performances, The Sink attracts generations of alumni and celebrities, The Fitter sells glass pipes, and records can still be purchased at Albums on The Hill. Parking can be problematic, especially when the football team is at home. A CU hotel and conference center and a new hotel are scheduled to be completed in 2025 and 2023, respectively. Each will bring additional merchants and accommodations into the area.

Fox Theatre
1135 13th St., 303-447-0095
z2ent.com/fox-theatre-venue

The Sink
1165 13th St., 303-444-7465
thesink.com

The Fitter
1121 13th St., 303-442-4200
thefitterboulder.com

Albums on The Hill
1128 13th St., 303-447-0159
bouldercoloradousa.com/listings/albums-on-the-hill/2640

Limelight Hotel Boulder
colorado.edu/today/2021/12/06/limelight-hotels-cu-
boulder-partnering-develop-campus-conference-center-hotel

The Hill Hotel
thehillboulder.com/hill-hotel

General Information Regarding The Hill
thehillboulder.com

STAND
SHOULDER TO SHOULDER
BY PURCHASING
CU BUFFS APPAREL
AT THE CU BOOKSTORE

Game day mandates wearing CU Buffs attire. Hands down, the CU Bookstore in the University Memorial Center offers the best selection of CU black and gold paraphernalia. This store has the latest CU Buffs gear ranging from the typical T-shirt to tailgate gear. The CU insignia, along with its buffalo mascot, Ralphie, are emblazoned on almost everything imaginable—tops, pants and shorts, jackets, sweatshirts, socks, hats, gloves, scarfs, keychains, household goods, sporting equipment, pet supplies, license-plate frames, stuffed animals, and gifts for CU graduates. The closest covered parking lot is the Euclid Parking Garage at 1795 Euclid Ave. Small kiosks are available at football and basketball games and other CU-sponsored events. Don't leave Boulder without at least one Ralphie souvenir.

University Memorial Center
1669 Euclid Ave., 303-492-6411
cubookstore.com

TAKE HOME
A PIECE OF COLORADO
FROM BOCO LIFE LLC

Friends and acquaintances mingle in this old-fashioned retail shop, where Paula Johansen instills camaraderie between her staff and customers. Breezy, the store's mascot, greets visitors. This family-run business offers a hospitable environment where people walking into the store feel at home. While mom and dad shop, children can color and play with toys. The products have one thing in common: a Boulder or Colorado theme. These destination products include ordinary licensed items singling out sports teams—CU, the Broncos, the Avalanche, the Nuggets, and the Rockies. Products made in Boulder, Fort Collins, Loveland, Denver, and Durango are showcased in the local section. With one of the best selections of Colorado-themed merchandise, take time to pick your favorites so you can remember your visit for years to come.

1615 Pearl St., 303-386-4638
shopboco.life

SELECT A BOOK
AT THE BOULDER BOOK STORE

Booklovers and historians will be intrigued by this Boulder icon. David Bolduc founded the Boulder Book Store in 1973 to satisfy the diverse needs of locals and visitors. The remodeled 19th-century building houses more than 100,000 titles displayed on three spacious and well-designed floors. Not surprisingly, it is Boulder's largest independent bookstore. With the assistance of the store's knowledgeable and personable staff, it is easy to locate your top choices, including used books, and to order out-of-print books. Rounding out the impressive inventory are gift items created by local artisans and manufacturers. Shopping local is a dominant theme. Check the website for upcoming special events, usually held in the upstairs ballroom. Hundreds of speakers, from best-sellers to first-time authors, visit each year.

1107 Pearl St., 303-447-2074
boulderbookstore.net

MAINTAIN YOUR ADVENTUROUS SPIRIT
WITH ACTIVE IMPRINTS FOOTWEAR

Just off the Pearl Street Mall you can visit Active Imprints, a family-owned business run by Danny and Jennifer Abshire. Their goal is to assist world-class triathletes, runners, skiers, and climbers, as well as everyday people, in staying active and performing at their best capacity without foot, knee, or hip pain. If you forget to pack comfortable shoes, this is one place to check out. For more than 30 years, they have been designing footwear and fabricating custom orthotics onsite. They sell their own brand, ACTIVE88 Footwear, which has been keeping people active since 1988. While in the store, check out their number-one shoe design featuring a Colorado Flag logo. Their motto is Minimal by design. Maximum protection. Paintings and custom leatherwork are also available.

1926 14th St., 303-494-0321
activeimprintsco.com

TAKE CARE OF YOUR PET
AT FARFEL'S FARM & RESCUE

Farfel's Farm & Rescue, a dog and cat boutique store on Pearl Street, is well known for its rescue program, which matches rescued dogs with local owners. Locals and visitors shop for high-quality dog and cat foods and supplies. The emphasis is on Colorado-based products not usually available at large pet-food chain stores. Top-selling treats come from Colorado-based Pawsitively Gourmet, a family-owned Boulder dog-food company specializing in nutritional pet food, and Winnie Lou, a local food truck and treat company for dogs. Pawsitively Gourmet's heart-shaped treat with a Colorado flag is hands down the most popular. Pet owners looking for a way to calm their pets find comfort in Suzie's CBD treats. This family-owned company sells third-party, lab-tested certified organic products for dogs and cats.

906 Pearl St., 303-443-7711
farfels.com

SHOP FOR BOTANICALS
AT REBECCA'S HERBAL
APOTHECARY & SUPPLY

Rebecca's Herbal Apothecary was founded in 2004 as a resource for learning more about herbs and a place to purchase natural products without additives. This store met the growing needs of Boulderites who were adopting a healthier lifestyle with an emphasis on nutrient-dense organic foods and the use of botanicals. Shoppers will immediately notice the aroma emanating from the assortment of plant-based products and the immense number of items that are prepared onsite in the apothecary's commercial kitchen. Some customers shop for cooking herbs and special teas, while others are interested in purchasing natural ingredients to make their own bath and body preparations. Most of the store's ready-made bath and body products are made onsite. Prepackaged bags and boxes are great gift items. The herbalists share their experiences as well as traditional uses for herbs. Online and in-person classes are informative.

1227 Spruce St., 303-443-8878
rebeccasherbs.com

BUY A KITE
FROM INTO THE WIND KITES

It is not uncommon to experience winds between 60 and 100 miles per hour in Boulder County. While such high-speed winds can be dangerous and are too extreme for kite flying, less windy days are perfect. Since 1980, Into the Wind has designed an impressive array of creative kites for people to enjoy in Boulder and elsewhere. Young and old wander through the Pearl Street Mall store gazing at the colorful kites designed to fly in conditions ranging from zero wind to 30 miles per hour, with higher-end kites handing winds of up to 60 miles per hour. From do-it-yourself kite kits to sophisticated stunt kites to decorative wind art, along with hard-to-find games and toys, the store covers all the bases.

1408 Pearl St., 303-449-5906
intothewind.com

BRING HOME A PIECE OF BOULDER HISTORY
FROM ART SOURCE INTERNATIONAL

It is fitting that a store selling antique maps and historic prints is in a century-old building on Boulder's historic downtown mall. History buffs could spend hours combing through the extensive collection of maps, photos, prints, and reproductions. The prime draw for this store is its impressive collection of original maps dating from the 15th century. More price-conscious shoppers will settle for a reproduction. Those wanting to bring home a piece of Colorado history will gravitate to the Colorado photo section, which features depictions of life from the end of the Civil War to the 1940s in more than 50 towns spread throughout the state. These black-and-white gems capture the essence of life during simpler times. Posters highlighting Colorado life today are also available.

1237 Pearl St., 303-444-4080
artsourceinternational.com

CHECK OUT CUSTOM GLASS PIPES
AT THE FITTER

Nearly 40 years before Colorado voters approved Amendment 64 in 2012 legalizing the production, sale, and use of recreational marijuana for adults, Bruce Klahr opened The Pipefitter, Boulder's first full-scale pipe shop. This hippy-era store attracted college students looking for wood and metal pipes, plastic and bamboo waterpipe bongs, black-light posters, lava lamps, mod clothing, and waterbeds. In 1975, Klahr sold the store to his twin sisters, Bonnie Dahl and Betty Gruskin, who at the time were recent college graduates. A government raid in 1991 and punitive government policies during President George W. Bush's administration caused economic setbacks and the renaming of the store to The Fitter. Nowadays, customers select from an assortment of glass hand pipes, scientific glass bongs, custom glassware created by artists, high tech vaporizers, and non–smoking-related items.

1121 13th St., 303-442-4200
thefitterboulder.com

ADMIRE ARTISANS
AT BOULDER ART GALLERIES

Since creative juices flow in spectacular natural settings, artists often migrate to the foothills of the Rockies. According to the National Endowment for the Arts, Boulder has the third-highest concentration of artists in the US, right behind Los Angeles and Santa Fe. The Boulder Art Association was formed as a nonprofit organization to support the work of beginning, emerging, and professional artists by sponsoring art shows, exhibits, and competitions, and to find ways to include visual arts in events throughout Boulder. Members include independent artists as well as storefronts. Their galleries display a cross section of local, regional, national, and international artistic endeavors including sculptures, glasswork, woodwork, pottery, windchimes, jewelry, photography, prints, and paintings. Devote half a day to visiting a local art museum and some of these Boulder galleries.

15th Street Gallery
1708 15th St., 303-447-2841
15thstreetgalleryboulder.com

Mary Williams Fine Arts
5311 Western Ave., 303-938-1588
marywilliamsfinearts.com

R Gallery
2027 Broadway St., 303-444-4146
rgallery.art

SmithKlein Gallery
1116 Pearl St., 303-444-7200
smithklein.com

Art & Soul Gallery
1505 Pearl St., 303-544-5803
artandsoulboulder.com

Boulder Art Association
boulderartassociation.org

SELECT HANDCRAFTED JEWELRY
AT A SPECIALTY JEWELRY STORE

Nationwide chain stores are okay for ordinary gifts, but several downtown Boulder stores are a good bet for unique pieces. Using raw diamonds, Todd Reed has rebranded the idea of luxury in his one-of-a-kind, hand-forged pieces using classic and modern metalsmithing techniques. Angela Olsgard Tiernan works directly with customers to produce ethically sourced pieces created from metals and gems. Beginning as the first woman Boulder bench jeweler in the 1970s, Linda Kozloff-Turner eventually created her own custom jewelry studio, Christine Marguerite Designs. Early on, she acquired the skills to saw metal, solder the pieces, set stones, and finish the job at the bench. If you don't mind waiting a few months, J. Albrecht Designs will personally design a custom piece, or you can select from the J. Albrecht Collection. Hurdle's Jewelry has the distinction of having opened in 1947. They sell personalized jewelry and items created by national designers.

Todd Reed
1911 Pearl St., 303-442-6280
toddreed.com

Angie Star Jewelry
1807 Pearl St., 720-565-0288
angiestarjewelry.com
Another location in Fort Collins

Christine Marguerite Designs
1942 Broadway St., Ste. 407, 303-447-2344
christinemarguerite.com

J. Albrecht Designs/Master Goldsmiths
951 Pearl St., 303-543-9191
jalbrechtdesigns.com

Hurdle's Jewelry
1402 Pearl St., 303-443-1084
hurdlesjewelry.com

GEAR UP
FOR YOUR NEXT ADVENTURE

Whether you are engaging in an active mountain adventure or taking a leisurely stroll along Boulder Creek, comfortable shoes are essential gear. Check out Boulder Running Company, Pedestrian Shops, and In Motion Running for shoes and boots to handle all terrains. In Boulder, well-known national and international brands permeate the marketplace, but you can find independent mountain adventure stores whose knowledgeable staff have hands-on experience. Even though Neptune Mountaineering has changed ownership numerous times, it has been operating in Boulder since 1973. Functional as well as unique backpacks, cross-body totes, purses, and travel gear can be purchased at By Elke and Sherpani, two woman-owned companies that take pride in designing their products in Boulder. Eye protection is essential on sunny Colorado days and when engaging in mountain adventures. Boulder-based Zeal Optics encourages customers to explore the world by wearing the best optics available.

Neptune Mountaineering
633 S Broadway St., 303-499-8866
neptunemountaineering.com

By Elke
4593 N Broadway, 720-535-9531
byelke.com

Sherpani
1711 Pearl St., 720-938-8299
sherpani.com

Pedestrian Shops
1425 Pearl St., 303-449-5260
2525 Arapahoe Ave., 303-449-7440
comfortableshoes.com

In Motion Running
1880B 30th St., 720-808-7232
inmotionrunning.com

Boulder Running Company
2775 Pearl St., 303-939-8000
Additional Stores in Denver, Littleton,
and Greenwood Village
fleetfeet.com/s/denverboulder

Zeal Optics
1230 Spruce St., 303-449-9322
zealoptics.com

IMPROVE YOUR BRAIN FUNCTION
WITH A LIBERTY PUZZLE

Assembling a large jigsaw puzzle can engage a family for days. Liberty Puzzles takes this tradition back to an earlier time, before the pieces were die-cut and constructed of flimsy cardboard. In 2005, Sage Wirth, Chris Wirth, and Jeff Eldridge founded Liberty Puzzles and started creating sturdy wooden puzzle pieces. They were the first company to cut the puzzle pieces with a laser and incorporate unique, whimsical pieces throughout the puzzle design. Working with local artists, they have produced Colorado-themed puzzles featuring the Flatirons, Colorado flags, bison, and bears. With more than 700 images available online and approximately 150 rotating styles in the Boulder store, Liberty offers puzzle lovers an abundance of ready-made choices. Individuals seeking a custom design can special order their unique puzzle.

Liberty Puzzles
1468 Pearl St., 720-524-6082
2526 49th St., 303-444-1442
Please check the website for Factory and Showroom reopening dates.
libertypuzzles.com

ACTIVITIES
BY SEASON

SPRING

SUMMER

• •

FALL

• •

WINTER

• •

SUGGESTED
ITINERARIES

ONLY IN BOULDER

OUTSIDE BOULDER

• •

DOWNTOWN AREA

• •

• •

● ●

EXPAND YOUR HORIZON

AT YOUR LEISURE

ROMANTIC ENCOUNTERS

• •

STAND SHOULDER TO SHOULDER
WITH THE BUFFALOES

INDEX